The POTATO
HARVEST COOKBOOK

P9-EDM-640

The POTATO
HARVEST COOKBOOK

Ashley Miller

The Taunton Press

Taunton
BOOKS & VIDEOS
for fellow enthusiasts

Text © 1998 by Ashley Miller
Photos by Boyd Hagen and illustration on p. 13 © 1998
  by The Taunton Press, Inc.
All rights reserved.

Printed in the United States of America
10 9 8 7 6 5 4 3 2 1

The Taunton Press, Inc., 63 South Main Steet,
P.O. Box 5506, Newtown, CT 06470-5506
e-mail: tp@taunton.com

Distributed by Publishers Group West

Library of Congress Cataloging-in-Publication Data

Miller, Ashley (Ashley M.)
    The potato harvest cookbook / Ashley Miller.
        p.   cm.
    Includes bibliographical references and index.
    ISBN 1-56158-246-8
    1. Cookery (Potatoes). 2. Potatoes. I. Title.
TX803.P8M56   1998
641.6'521—dc21   97-48533
                                         CIP

For Gene, Eric, Jillian, and
Meredith,

who never met a spud they
didn't like,

who heard the music of the
tubers and
marched along.

ACKNOWLEDGMENTS

In a world that is increasingly hooked up to web sites, chat rooms, and CD-ROMs, I am increasingly grateful for libraries. Books will always have a satisfying reality for me that is embodied in their silence and materiality.

In an age when most library budgets are being apportioned to meet the demands for the constant and rapid increase in computer technology and services, a sojourn into a stack of books is a pleasure intensified by the fact that it may become a rarity. The immense wealth of inspiration and information to be found in the stacks of Mann Library at Cornell University is a resource for which I am always grateful. Access to this collection has consistently been aided by Mann Library's superb and accommodating staff.

Located in a town that takes cooking seriously, Ithaca's Tompkins County Library takes great pains to maintain an extensive and varied cookbook collection. I have been a steady customer in that department and would like to express my thanks for this inspiring public resource.

David Cavagnaro's contribution to this book is obvious in his vision and talent as a photographer. What may not be so evident is his extraordinary horticultural knowledge stemming from years of dedicated gardening, a resource he shares with great generosity and good humor and for which I am immensely grateful.

At The Taunton Press, Cherilyn DeVries has been my sounding board and valued advisor. Her encouragement, thoughtful suggestions, and ever-ready wit have added immeasurably to this book.

Christina Stark has gone above and beyond her duties as a nutritionist for Cornell Cooperative Extension, not only cheerfully digging into her extensive network of information when faced with my numerous questions but also sending me articles collected while on vacation. I am grateful for her up-to-the-minute knowledge, commitment to education, and marvelous sense of humor.

To Connie Welch, who tested every recipe in this book, my heartfelt thanks for clarifying and fine-tuning them.

It is an immense pleasure to have my text appear in such a beautifully designed and produced book. Thanks to Jodie Delohery for her handsome design and high standards and to Boyd Hagen for his wide-ranging talents and abilities as a photographer.

My gratitude to Joan Ormondroyd, a fabulous cook and treasured friend, is tremendous. Her aid with the recipes, as well as her culinary and emotional sustenence, is greatly appreciated.

For kindly imparting their hard-won potato expertise, I would like to thank Megan Gerritsen of Wood Prairie Farms, Alison LaCourse of Moose Tubers, and Jerry Goodman and Sue Lutovsky of Ronnigers.

And finally, my heartfelt gratitude to Gene Endres, Louise Miller, Meredith Broberg, Eric Broberg, and Jillian Hull for their unwavering support and creative and critical contributions.

CONTENTS

INTRODUCTION

Ten years ago, I moved from a small house in town with a tiny but productive vegetable garden to a home in the country with a vast overarching sky and an equally vast space for a garden. This new space meant stands of tall corn; wandering, unruly winter squashes; and, most exciting, rows and rows of potatoes. Visions of freshly harvested diminutive new potatoes came to mind and quickly multiplied into a winter's worth, stored in the stone stairway beneath my cellar door and lying quietly in wait to be turned into an unlimited variety of comforting dishes.

Growing these earth apples, as the French call them, is like growing no other vegetable. I dig a trench and toss small or cut-up potatoes into it, shovel dirt over them, and walk away. Tiny, wrinkled green leaves appear from a crack in the earth, rapidly increasing until a plant is formed. This plant grows lush and radiates a constellation of starry blossoms. But the main event is happening in secret, underground. In the dark of the earth, tips of subterranean stems are swelling and forming themselves into dense and fleshy tubers. This is the transformation that I have waited for. On a sunny day in early autumn, I reach for the digging fork and proceed to the spent-looking potato bed. At the beginning of a row, I plunge the fork in. With the fork's initial lift is a revelation of buried treasure. I marvel at this array of earthy nuggets still jacketed in a thin layer of soil and once again smile with a vision of satisfying and savory eating.

What I am harvesting is the most important vegetable in the world. At present, the potato is the fourth-largest food crop on the planet, following wheat, corn, and rice. Its adaptability to wildly varied growing conditions and its high yield per acre account for this importance. Although the potato grows best in moist, temperate regions, it can grow on the slopes of 12,000-ft. mountains, in areas of scant rainfall and marginal soil, and in climates of little warmth and sun. It is a nutritious vegetable, containing significant amounts of vitamins C and B_6, niacin, iron, and potassium. Although we may think of the potato in culinary and nutritional terms, its great versatility has been turned to many uses: alcohol, used in World War I explosives and anesthetics and today as vodka; starch, used as a thickener and in early color photography; flour; glucose; animal fodder; dyes; perfumes; and, of course, ammo for the ever-popular Spud Gun.

If power is derived from economic or spiritual sources, then potatoes are powerful. Suggestions of ritual mutilation and sacrifice to ensure a plentiful crop can be found in ancient Andean ceramics. In this country, potatoes are a $6.1 billion business. Of the entire U.S. harvest, more than 70% of potatoes are processed, mostly into the ubiquitous chips and fries but also dehydrated into such products as instant mashed, boxed scalloped, and microwavable hash-browned potatoes. Unfortunately, the more a potato is processed, the more its price goes up and its nutritional value goes down.

In the not-too-distant past, potatoes only came in white and were considered fattening. This began to change in the mid-1980s with the introduction of the delectable, yellow-fleshed Yukon Gold and increasing interest in the wealth of flavor and forms found in heirloom varieties. Today, the range of colors that can be found in potatoes would have been unimaginable to the shirtwaisted, high-heeled housewife of the 1950s. In addition to yellow-fleshed varieties, potatoes can be had in shades of purple or pink. You can also buy appealing fingerlings, tasty and dense keepers with intriguing names such as Russian Banana and Swedish Peanut.

As for potatoes being fattening, The Potato Board has straightened us out on that one. A medium, 5½-ounce potato that has been baked, steamed, or boiled contains about 145 calories. For comparison, 1 cup of mixed salad greens with 2 tablespoons of a homemade vinaigrette has 150 calories. It's what we choose for toppings and how they're cooked that have given potatoes their fatty reputation. Plop ¼ cup of sour cream atop that naked baked potato and you nearly double the calorie count.

A cooked potato can be a simple and comforting end in itself, or it can be the beginning of a sublimely memorable dish. As the most versatile vegetable of all, potatoes are delicious mashed, hashed, baked, boiled, steamed, roasted, riced, and diced. Their neutrality of flavor makes them ideal candidates for combining with other foods, and they take well to a variety of herbs and spices. With all this going for them, it is not difficult to create potato dishes that are high in taste and low in fat.

In an early chapter of *How to Cook a Wolf*, written by M. F. K. Fisher during the dark days of World War II, she begins with a quote from J. T. Pettee, a 19th-century American writer:

> "Pray for peace and grace and spiritual food,
> For wisdom and guidance, for all these are good,
> But don't forget the potatoes."

Yes, let us not forget the potatoes.

Buried Treasure

When the Spanish invaded Peru in the early 16th century, they were looking for one thing—gold. They obtained the much-desired gold, which was melted and hauled back to Spain, but left unrecorded was the gain of booty whose importance and value has far exceeded all of the gold taken from the New World. This was the potato.

This succulent, starchy lump is now the most important of all vegetables, ranking only behind the grains wheat, corn, and rice in worldwide value. In the United States, potatoes are big business: in 1996, the crop brought in $2.5 billion, and the average American downed 142 pounds of them. Not bad for a plant originally rejected by Europeans as being poisonous.

This initial prejudice was caused by the fact that the potato is a member of the *Solanum* family, which in the words of John Ruskin, the English critic, is "a tribe set aside for evil, having the deadly nightshade for its queen, and including the henbane, witches mandrake, and the worst natural curse of civilization, tobacco." There you have the notorious side of the family. However, favorites of the summer garden—tomatoes, eggplants, and peppers—are likewise *Solanaceae* whose reputations were also initially tarnished by their poisonous relatives.

The etymology of potatoes provides some fascinating examples of unrestrained linguistic leaps. In its land of origin, the potato was (and still is) called the "papa," which was duly recorded by early Spanish chroniclers who often compared it to another underground edible, the truffle. The tie to truffles took hold in Italy, where as early as 1584 potatoes were known as "tartuffo," a derivative of the Italian word for truffle. This name was converted to "cartoufle" by the French and to "kartoffel" by the Germans as it made its way into western Europe.

A group portrait of the world's most important vegetable, Solanum tuberosum.

Other members of the Solanum *or Nightshade family that were initially greeted with suspicion in Europe are tomatoes, eggplants, peppers, and tomatillos.*

In England, the potato's resemblance to another New World tuber resulted in its "potato" designation. The common potato was assumed to be a permutation of the sweet potato, an earlier arrival introduced to England from Spain that was called "batata" or "patata." With an agriculture based on seeds, Europeans were unfamiliar with tuberous vegetables, so their linking of the sweet potato (*Ipomea batata*) with the common potato (*Solanum*

Potatoes grow underground and are thought of as a root vegetable, but botanically they are defined as stem tubers, an underground stem swollen with carbohydrates, protein, and water. (Courtesy of Corbis-Bettmann.)

tuberosum) is understandable. Thus, the potato made its debut in the English language under the alias of a completely different plant.

LOOK A POTATO IN THE EYE

Although potatoes are generally termed root vegetables, botanists quickly point out that they are not roots. The edible part of the potato plant is actually a stem tuber, an underground stem swollen with carbohydrates, protein, and water, whose purpose is strictly reproductive. The flowers of a potato will occasionally produce a small, seed-bearing poisonous berry, but typically these flowers are sterile. If you look a potato in the eye, you will see the dormant buds of a new plant. The starch that we happily consume baked, boiled, or fried is the storehouse that nourishes the future plant until its sprouting buds develop true roots to absorb nutrients and moisture from the soil.

A closer look at a potato brings more revelations: on one end, you will notice a neat, circular scar, sometimes with a bit of dried stem. This is where the potato was attached to the underground stem of its parent plant. At the opposite end, you will observe a cluster of eyes that spread out and wind around the potato. These are arranged in a spiral, the mystical and orderly growth form found throughout nature.

THE PERFECT FOOD

As The Potato Board has spent millions to let us know, potatoes are far from fattening. They are low in calories, have no cholesterol, and have almost no fat. It's how they're cooked and what they're topped with that quickly ratchets up these numbers. A 5½-ounce baked potato contains only 145 calories. When you add ¼ cup of sour cream or a tablespoon of butter, you add not only at least 100 calories but also saturated fat and cholesterol.

The relatively low calorie content of potatoes comes from the fact that they, like most vegetables, contain almost no fat. Nearly all of the calories come from beneficial complex carbo-

Blame the toppings, not the potato itself, for this high-fat dish.

NUTRIENT VALUES FOR VARIOUS POTATO PREPARATIONS

As any nutritionist will tell you, the less a food is processed, the more nutrients it retains. To illustrate this point, compare these nutrient numbers for several types of potato preparations.

Potato Type	Calories	Protein	Vitamin C	Potassium	Sodium	Saturated Fat
One 5½-oz. baked potato, flesh only	145	3.06g	20mg	610mg	8mg	0.041g
French fries, frozen and fried in vegetable oil (1 cup)	180	2.3g	5.9g	417mg	123mg	2.84g
Mashed with whole milk, margarine, and salt (1 cup)	222	3.95g	12.9mg	607mg	619mg	2.17g
Dehydrated mashed, prepared with whole milk and butter (1 cup)	237	4g	20.4mg	490mg	697mg	7.21g
Potato chips (1-oz. serving, about 14 chips)	148	1.82mg	11.8mg	369mg	133mg	2.57g

Source: U.S. Department of Agriculture (USDA)

hydrates and protein. The protein in potatoes is considered high quality with a good balance of amino acids, which are the protein building blocks that must be provided in the diet to enable our bodies to completely utilize the protein we eat. Potatoes also have an unusually high amount of vitamin C, which led to their use as a scurvy preventative by Spanish sailors and Alaskan gold miners.

A new 5-ounce potato supplies more than half the recommended daily amount of vitamin C, although this vitamin decreases as potatoes are stored. Significant amounts of potassium, iron, niacin, and vitamin B_6 demonstrate why this comforting and versatile vegetable is often described as "the perfect food."

FRIES AND CHIPS

The first potatoes grown in this country traveled not overland from their Andean cradle but over the Atlantic from their adoptive home in the British Isles. Speculation on the first growers usually points to a group of Scotch-Irish who settled in Derry, New Hampshire, in 1719. The distance between that first modest potato harvest on our shores and the current global presence of french fries and potato chips is a story of American inventiveness, capitalistic enterprise, and scientific and technological excellence. The current chapter of cultural domination, an unpopular one in many countries, is symbolized by the rapidly expanding numbers of overseas American fast food outlets. The largest and most successful of these,

POTATO NOVELTIES

Spuds give us nourishing and comforting food, have thousands of years of history, and are the most important vegetable crop in the world. They also furnish amusement.

Mr. Potato Head

When the children's plaything Mr. Potato Head first appeared in 1952, it was a simple kit of plastic facial features and accessories that you stuck into an actual potato. Not long afterward, symbol was substituted for reality as a 1-in. slab of vaguely potato-shaped Styrofoam appeared with the stick-on features. Since then Mr. Potato Head has acquired a grotesque new plastic head and body. He has a wife and children, had a role in a popular Disney movie, and can now be found on your computer screen—virtual Mr. Potato Head.

Potato pistols

The eighth most popular item at Archie McPhee's, a Seattle-based novelty emporium, is a Spud Gun, a pseudo-pistol that shoots potato pellets. Potatoes are connected to another pseudo-pistol that enabled the notorious criminal John Dillinger to escape from jail. Purportedly, he carved a small pistol from a large potato, blacked it with shoe polish, and bluffed his way out of jail. At the other extreme of spud weaponry are spud cannons. These potentially dangerous missiles are concocted, usually by teenage boys, of PVC pipe, a gas-grill igniter, and hairspray and are capable of blasting a potato at high speed for several hundred yards.

Tater batteries

If two dissimilar metal wires (for example, one copper and one zinc) are stuck into a potato, an electrolytic reaction produces a bit of low-voltage electricity. I've always imagined a potato-powered kitchen as a prime example of appropriate technology.

McDonald's, peddles two main products that have become synonymous with America—burgers and fries.

Language can often be used as a reliable guide to changes within a society. The etymology of french fries is a case in point, as it reflects the ever increasing industrialization of our food. When Thomas Jefferson returned to this country after a stint as ambassador to France, he brought back a great appreciation for many aspects of French culture, particularly its cuisine. In his graceful dining room at Monticello, he often served "Potatoes Fried in the French Manner" to other members of the Virginia plantation aristocracy. With the passage of time, this dish became known as "French Fried Potatoes," then in the 1920s was further shortened to "French frieds." This abbreviation coincided with the introduction of a technical improvement—a mechanical potato peeler that paved the way for increased production and wider availability of this popular treat. By the next decade, "french fries," were still French but demoted to a lower case "f". Today, the reference to their country of origin has been jettisoned, as "Potatoes Fried in the French Manner" have been transformed into a thoroughly Americanized entity, a fast-food product. Reflecting both the presence of fast food in the lives of most Americans and the time pressures on both employees and patrons of these establishments, Jefferson's sophisticated French introduction has become the inglorious "fries."

In contrast to fries, the origin of the potato chip is undeniably American and can be traced to the summer resort town of Saratoga

Crisp and tasty these are, but with processing the nutrition in a potato goes down while the fat, salt, additives, and price go up.

Springs, New York. In 1853, George Crum, an American Indian chef at Moon's Lake Lodge, ran into a difficult customer who kept sending his fried potatoes back to the kitchen with the complaint that they were too thick. Finally, an exasperated Crum put an end to the matter by producing a fried potato that was too thin and too crisp to eat with a fork. The result was an immediate success, and for years afterward "Saratoga chips" were a specialty of the house. As with french fries, the invention of the mechanical potato peeler in the 1920s greased the skids for the transformation of the potato chip into a nationally marketed snack.

As a visit to the local fast food outlet or supermarket clearly demonstrates, the consumption of fries and chips in this country is stupendous. A recent study reported that nearly one-quarter of the vegetables eaten by Americans ages 2 to 18 were french fries. Potatoes are a nutritious vegetable, but with processing the nutrition goes down and the fat, salt, additives, and price go up. By the time you hold that clever little cardboard container of fries in your hands, the potatoes have been cooked twice and frozen once.

Potatoes are also processed by dehydrating, an industrial remnant of World War II's easily stored and transported Army rations. Dehydrated potatoes in the form of instant mashed, hash browns, and scalloped potatoes all have less nutrition and more fat and sodium when prepared according to package directions than the same dishes made with "real" potatoes. Convenience always has a price, and in this country, the demand for convenience is huge. In recent years, at least 70% of the potato harvest is processed, of which an estimated 1 billion tons are processed for the retail market and another 7 billion tons for the food service industry.

One of the biggest trends in the food manufacturing industry is what is known as "home replacement meals," which are foods associated with the warmth and comfort of home cooking. And since the food industry knows that mashed potatoes top many people's lists of comfort foods, it is working night and day to come up with frozen microwavable or boil-in-a-bag mashed potatoes. Thanksgiving dinner may never be the same.

The Potato
in History

A recently colorized woodcut from a 1613 account of the daily life of the Inca shows the harvesting of potatoes. (Courtesy of The Granger Collection, New York.)

A potato blooms in the Andes, where they were first domesticated at least 7,000 years ago.

I t is an obvious truth that food is the substance that fuels the human race. This is as true today as it was 50,000 years ago, when humanity's quest for sustenance helped to shape the development of society. In the intertwined chronicle of the world's food and people, the potato stands out as a powerful force. This lumpish tuber has fueled population growth, effected a famine and economic collapse, caused vast migrations, and played a role in the outcome of wars.

SOUTH AMERICAN ORIGINS

The story of the potato begins in the mysterious grandeur of the south-central Andes at least 7,000 years ago. It was here that early planters are believed to have first domesticated the tuber that has become one of the most important food crops in the world. The value of the potato to the dwellers of this cold and exposed region was twofold. Since potatoes could be successfully grown at high elevations where corn, the staple of warmer meso-America, would not mature, their cultivation helped to form a base for a dependable food supply. This enabled populations to exist at extremely high elevations where eventually, in Peru and Bolivia, these settlements developed into some of the most advanced civilizations in the Americas. Of equal importance was, and still is, that by freeze-drying, this long-lasting staple could be preserved and stored for years as protection against famine. Because of their

Potatoes remain an important food throughout the highlands of South America, and many varieties can be seen at local markets. (Photo by Mike Irwin.)

longevity and lightness, freeze-dried potatoes, or *chuño*, also figured prominently in vital pre-Colombian trade between the Andes and coastal regions.

Although we think of freeze-drying as a relatively recent development, it is an ancient method, and *chuño* is one of humanity's original dehydrated foods. The process used today differs little from that used centuries ago. At high altitudes in the Andes, the temperature can fluctuate from below freezing at night to 80°F during the day. In addition, the climate is dry during most of the year. These conditions enable natives to freeze-dry potatoes by spreading them out on the ground and leaving them to freeze at night. The next day they tread on the potatoes with bare feet to expel water. This is repeated for several days until there is no more liquid to expel. They are then dried and stored for use in stews or ground into flour.

That potatoes possessed a social, and perhaps a sacred, significance can be seen in the remarkable pre-Incan ceramics of coastal Peru. There are many vessels in the form of a potato or with potato-like characteristics, such as a surface treatment of incised potato eyes. Other ceramic examples show potatoes with human features. Some of these have human faces with the upper lip and nose removed, which results in a mouth that bears a morbid resemblance to the eye of a potato. It is not known whether this mutilation was connected to an agricultural ritual to ensure a good harvest or whether it was simply a form of punishment meted out to miscreants or enemies.

EASTWARD HO

The first transport of potatoes across the Atlantic is unrecorded, although hospital records from Seville suggest that they were being grown in Spain by 1573. Their introduction into northern Europe is surrounded by controversy. Legend attributes their European debut to both Sir Francis Drake and Sir Walter Raleigh. Raleigh may have had something to do with the early cultivation of the potato in Ireland, where he had large estates, but he would have to share the credit. Some historians believe that the first potatoes in Ireland floated ashore from ships' provisions of the wrecked Spanish Armada in 1588. Another hypothesis has Basque fishermen, whose families were believed to be the first Europeans to grow potatoes, bringing the potato into Ireland when they dried their catch on shore before returning to northern Spain.

Like its relative the tomato, the potato did not leap into instant popularity in Europe. As a member of the nightshade family, it suffered from the popular belief that all members of that family were poisonous. The fact that greened or improperly stored potatoes can produce alkaloid poisoning would have affirmed this. This peculiar and foreign tuber was suspected of causing leprosy and scrofula and was widely thought to be an aphrodisiac, a belief stemming from its resemblance to the sweet potato, which was reputed to have erotic power. The common potato did play a part in a European population boom of the late 18th and early 19th century—but not as an aphrodisiac. In addition to being an easier crop to grow and harvest, an acre of highly nutritious potatoes could feed at least four times as many people as an acre of wheat. With the subject of this population explosion comes the most tragic chapter in the history of the potato.

THE GREAT FAMINE

In 1845, the Emerald Isle had a population in excess of 8 million, an increase of 142% within three generations. This stupendous growth,

Pre-Incan inhabitants of Peru often made vessels that resembled potatoes.

A 16th-century woodcut depicts the potato plant that originated in South America. (Courtesy of The Granger Collection, New York.)

LAZYBEDS

In Ireland, potatoes were cultivated in what the English disdainfully dubbed "lazybeds." A lazybed was so-called because the ground was not plowed or harrowed. To initiate a lazybed, a strip of ground, which ranged from 2 ft. wide in wet soils to 4 ft. wide in drier soils, was spread with whatever organic mulch was available—seaweed, dry peat, or manure. The seed potatoes were laid on top of the mulch and covered with pieces of sod dug up from trenches on either side of the mulched strip.

As the plants grew, they were hilled up with more dirt from the trenches. In effect, these were raised beds with ditches between them, which allowed excess rain to drain away and freezing air to flow downward. This system, as well as the shape of the specialized narrow shovel used, was remarkably similar to that used for centuries in Peru.

A closer look at the lazybed method reveals it to be a successful and ingenious adaptation to centuries of wholesale political and economic abuse by the English. As a result of government policies, many of which were inspired by a deep anti-Catholic bias, Irish farmers were driven off their arable lands and onto the poorer hillsides and bogs. The vast majority of rural inhabitants were tenants with small plots on large estates who were at the mercy of often absentee landlords.

The lazybed system was uniquely suited to overcoming the difficulties of cultivation on these agriculturally unsuitable lands. An entire crop could also be stored in the bed, thus doing away with the need for storage facilities and keeping the potatoes out of reach of voracious English troops. In this way, the potato became the staple of an oppressed population.

which occurred primarily among the rural poor, is attributed to the widespread cultivation of the potato, or "pratie" as it's often known in Ireland. Potatoes, supplemented with milk, formed nutritional fare to which even the poorest had access. And in Ireland's subsistence economy, there were many poor.

Historically, the Irish had taken to the potato in a way that no other Europeans had. By 1693, it had become so completely associated with the country that it was referred to as the "Irish Potato." Ireland's cool, moist climate and peaty, acidic soils provided ideal potato-growing conditions. In addition, a small plot of "lazybeds" in which the potatoes were cultivated could yield enough to meet the needs of an entire family (see the sidebar above).

In 1845, prospects looked excellent for a substantial potato harvest. September, however, brought some disquieting reports of diseased plants in the Dublin area. In October, most of the crop was still in the ground and there were conflicting reports on how widespread the outbreaks of disease were. Even after the first harvest, the crop appeared to be a fair one. But this prospect was short-lived, as seemingly sound potatoes soon turned black with rot. Late blight had spread throughout Ireland.

When the disease struck, the cause was unknown. Late blight is a fungus characterized by the virulent speed of its spread. It begins when a few plants turn brown and die off, then in warm, moist weather, the blight can spread to a whole field within a week. By the second week, the field will be black and stinking. Nearly a century after the Potato Famine, an attempt was made to establish the source of this blight. Records show that in 1843, the blight had been recognized in the northeastern United States and Nova Scotia. Within two years, it would appear in a land whose people and economy completely depended upon the potato.

The harvest of 1845 was reduced by half. The harvest of 1846 was a total loss, and the following year it was greatly reduced. Those who sought what little aid was available were thwarted by the restrictive and punitive measures that came from London. For example, the infamous Gregory Clause of the 1847 Poor Relief Act stipulated that tenants must give up their homes and their land before they could be eligible for relief. This nasty piece of legislation and the inability of many tenants to pay rent led to mass evictions and dispossessed families. Starvation, cholera, typhoid, scurvy, insanity, and blindness from vitamin A deficiency were causes of great public suffering and misery.

The legacy of this famine was far reaching, as Ireland lost nearly one-third of its population. Between 1846 and 1851, more than

An acre planted with potatoes can feed at least four times as many people as an acre of grain.

A drawing from American cartoonist Thomas Nast depicts post-famine relief sent to Ireland from the United States. (Courtesy of Corbis-Bettmann.)

THE POTATO PLAN

In an effort to increase England's domestic food supplies during World War II, the Ministry of Food encouraged farmers to grow more potatoes. To convince the public to shovel in and do their part, the Potato Plan was put into effect. Here is an excerpt from a letter by Lord Woolton, Minister of Food, published in the The Times (London) on December 5, 1942:

"An Island at war must use to the full the food it produces at home—and it must grow the foods that will keep the nation fighting fit. That is why the farmers were asked to grow record crops of potatoes. There is no glut of potatoes: it would be sensible to talk of a glut of planes or tanks. But neither tanks nor guns nor potatoes are of any use unless we put them to use. Potatoes must go into action on the Food Front.

Let your patriotism direct your appetite: eat potatoes—and if you are a cook, learn new ways of serving them."

Here are some of the suggestions offered under the Potato Plan printed in The Times (London) on January 14, 1943:

1. Serve potatoes for breakfast three days a week.

2. Make your main dish a potato dish one day a week.

3. Refuse second helpings of other food until you've had more potatoes.

4. Serve potatoes in other ways than "plain boiled."

1.5 million people died and 1 million were forced to leave. Many emigrated to the United States, where their descendents have contributed immeasurably to American life and where bitterness against English policies of 150 years ago can still surface. In 1996, a New York City legislator introduced a bill before the state legislature to require public school history textbooks to describe the Irish Potato Famine as an English attempt at genocide.

TATERS IN THE TRENCHES

Images of warfare run more toward armed aggression than agriculture, yet the latter has played an important role in military maneuvers for millenia. As Napoleon put it, "An army travels on its stomach." Because the potato is filling, nutritious, easily prepared, keeps well, and has industrial uses, it has played some interesting and important roles in armed conflicts.

There was, for starters, the "Potato War," the name given to the standoff more formally known as the War of the Bavarian Succession. While the Austrian emperor Joseph II hemmed and hawed on the sidelines, Frederick the Great of Prussia and his superior force of troops settled in for the winter of 1777-78 in Bohemia and went to work consuming the resources of the enemy's country—mainly potatoes. This was, after all, the area of present-day Poland, still known as a major potato producer. Had these armies been on the move, the Prussians probably wouldn't have bothered with potatoes since it was far more efficient to requisition stores of grain that were ready and waiting in local barns. The fact that potatoes could be stored in the ground, out of view of marauding armies and inquisitive tax collectors, was an undeniable asset to European peasants.

In Europe during the World Wars, potatoes fed both the troops and the homefolks. During World War I, some observers attributed Germany's increased military and industrial strength to an exceedingly large potato harvest in 1915. The Germans not only fed their troops (and their horses) potatoes but also used them extensively in industry. Alcohol and acetone derived from potatoes were used directly in the war effort in the manufacture of explosives, anesthetics, and rubber, as well as in a multitude of vital, nonmilitary products.

Because an acre of potatoes can feed far more people than an acre of grain, England had a "Potato Plan." With straight face and stiff upper lip, the Potato and Carrot Division of the Ministry of Food administered the plan to increase England's food supplies during World War II (see the sidebar on the facing page). Potatoes were of such importance to the Germans that in 1939 Germany accused Britain of airlifting Colorado potato beetles to German fields in an effort to subvert the Third Reich.

OUR HUMBLE HERO

Looking at a potato does not stir the historical imagination. It has neither the beauty nor durability of finely worked metal. It lacks the resonance of a scrap of ancient paper with handwritten marks on it. It is what it is: an earthy, unprepossesing lump, often with the term "humble" affixed to it.

But why humble? This is the most important vegetable on the planet, a multibillion dollar tuber that is now making french-fried incursions into the traditional rice turf of Asia. This is the vegetable whose ability to produce at high altitudes enabled the advancement of the Andean cultures that culminated in one of the

The humble potato is an object of affection for millions.

world's great civilizations, the empire of the Inca. This is the vegetable whose failure to produce changed western history with the death and migration of 2.5 million people and whose prolific production in 1915 influenced Germany's World War I plans. With a *curriculum vitae* like this, "humble" seems an unlikely prefix for the potato.

And yet this vegetable, more than any other, is the one we take into our hearts and homes. Although we live in the wealthiest country in the world with a vast array of available edibles from which to choose, we select the potato. Unpretentious in looks, it offers substance instead. It comforts us with its simple integrity and undemanding nourishment, asking nothing, giving sustenance. In a word, humble.

A Gallery
of Potatoes

One might think that there is not much new about a staple that we have taken for granted for centuries. "As plain as a potato" is an aphorism that not only indicates that taters may be short on looks but also suggests their ubiquity. The increasing availability of unusual and definitely unplain potatoes, as well as their appearance in upscale restaurants and markets, may render this particular saying obsolete.

Cherished old varieties, such as Irish Cobbler and Green Mountain, are still around, but potato lovers now have a wealth of choices. Traditionalists firmly believe that the only color the inside of a potato should be is white, but the more adventurous can find potatoes with yellow, pink, or lavender-blue flesh. Potato skins can be had in wonderful hues with a wide range of contrasting swirls and markings. While this range of color and pattern may be new to us, the essence of the potato remains the same—they're great eating.

Potatoes, all of which carry the botanical name *Solanum tuberosum*, are categorized several ways depending on who's doing the categorizing. Cooks generally classify them according to starch content, produce managers according to shape and skin color, and growers according to the date a potato variety matures. Most garden catalogs use the latter system, listing varieties under early, midseason, and late with an additional category for fingerlings.

EARLY POTATOES
(70 DAYS OR LESS)
Early potatoes size up fast, which makes them ideal candidates for the season's first new potatoes. When planted early enough, their rapid initial growth often enables them to outrace insect problems that occur later in the season.

Although there are exceptions, early varieties are not known as great storage potatoes.

Bison
What a pleasure to unearth a clutch of these round, rose-red potatoes. This variety is productive and versatile, providing delicious, creamy new potatoes and, when dug at maturity, excellent storage potatoes. Bison is resistant to late blight and scab (see p. 38).

Caribe
A vivid red-purple skin and snowy white flesh make this a beautiful potato, but Caribe offers a lot more than looks. It sizes up early for new potatoes, has high yields, and produces well under stress. Other features are good storage qualities and moderate resistance to scab. Contrary to many reports, Caribe was not grown in New England for export to the Caribbean to feed slaves, nor was it grown in

Bison

Caribe

Charlotte

Chieftain

that tropical region. It is a 1984 release from AgCanada, that country's Department of Agriculture.

Charlotte

Charlotte produces a great deal of smooth-skinned, medium, oblong potatoes with delectable yellow flesh early in the season. It is best enjoyed fresh from the garden.

Chieftain

Chieftain is a high-yielding, all-purpose variety of lovely rosy-skinned potatoes. Excellent flavor and appearance make this a popular commercial variety, particularly for new potatoes. It is resistant to scab and late blight but has a relatively short storage life.

Dark Red Norland

Newly dug and washed, this potato is such a dazzling magenta that it makes a potato lover's heart go pitter-pat just looking at it. Dark Red Norlands are particularly creamy as new potatoes. If any make it to maturity, they are also a

good storage potato. This variety was selected for its brighter skin and high yields from Norland, a widely grown, slightly earlier red potato developed and released in North Dakota in 1957.

Frontier Russet

Frontier Russet is an early-maturing russet that makes it a good choice for gardeners with short growing seasons. This flaky-textured baking potato is a good producer of medium to large tubers with excellent flavor and keeping qualities. It is resistant to scab and verticillium wilt, as well as to a number of other diseases.

Irish Cobbler

This is a tater that has stood the test of time. Its name is believed to have come from a cobbler in New Jersey who grew it from seed sometime prior to 1885. Irish Cobbler is a reliable and widely adapted all-purpose potato that is usually the first to bloom in the potato patch. When harvested as new potatoes, this variety has skin so tender it barely stays on. Fresh use is

Dark Red Norland

Frontier Russet

Irish Cobbler

recommended; it has a short storage life. This old favorite, also known as Cobbler, is susceptible to verticillium wilt and scab.

Red Dale

Red Dale is a large, round, rose-pink potato with fine white flesh. This variety hails from Minnesota, where it was released in 1984. Besides good looks and flavor, Red Dale boasts high resistance to scab and verticillium wilt and is a good keeper. Red Dales should be planted 8 in. to 10 in. apart to control size.

Yukon Gold

The first of the yellow-fleshed types to hit the big time, Yukon Gold has become the favorite potato of many consumers and gardeners. Amongst the generic white, red, or baking potatoes found in supermarkets, Yukon Gold may be the only potato varietal name that shoppers are familiar with. This potato's delicious flesh is drier than that of other yellow varieties, which makes it great for baking and mashing. A 1980 release from AgCanada,

Red Dale

Yukon Gold

All Blue

Yukon Gold is an excellent producer of medium-to-large storage potatoes and is considered moderately susceptible to scab. Small pink eyes distinguish Yukon Gold from other yellow-fleshed potatoes.

MIDSEASON POTATOES (70 TO 90 DAYS)

These are slower-growing varieties that are most often planted as storage potatoes. Catalogs often refer to them as the "main crop" and recommend planting them two to three weeks later than early potatoes. This is so they can be harvested in cooler weather, then transferred to cool or cold storage areas, such as root cellars or other unheated spaces.

All Blue

All Blue is an extraordinary-looking potato with dark blue-violet skin and lavender-blue flesh. This potato was initially treated as a novelty, but its fine taste, productivity, and aesthetic appeal keep gardeners and cooks coming back for more. All Blue is great for baking or roasting (it is especially dramatic with golden beets flecked with dill) and makes a delicious, delicately tinted lavender salad. This variety is also known as Purple Marker, which alludes to its use in potato fields to separate different varieties. It has moderate resistance to scab and late blight.

All Red

All Red is a name that is easy to remember, but it is a bit of an exaggeration. This beauty actually has an interior of pale, delicate pink, a hue more reminiscent of a rose petal than a vegetable. All Red is considered the best producer of the red-skinned, red-fleshed varieties and gives good yields of medium, round, low-starch potatoes.

Carola

Carola, also known as Carole, was introduced from Germany in 1979 and has become a favorite of many gardeners. It offers a lot: fine taste, moist and creamy-textured yellow flesh, high yields, and good storage qualities. It is highly resistant to scab and moderately resistant to late blight.

All Red

Carola

Goldrush

Goldrush

Goldrush is a russet potato introduced in 1992 from breeding efforts at the University of North Dakota. Although primarily a commercial variety, it offers the home grower medium-to-large, exceptionally white-fleshed tubers with fine flavor. The plants show good resistance to scab and drought but are susceptible to early and late blight.

Kennebec

Kennebec bears the name of a river and a town in Maine. Introduced in 1948, Kennebec is a good all-purpose variety that does well under a wide range of soil conditions. This potato is drought-tolerant and resistant to late blight. Kennebec can produce very large potatoes, so to control their size, an 8-in. to 10-in. spacing when planting is recommended.

Pinto

In Spanish, *pinto* comes from a verb that means "to paint." One look at this color-splashed spud reveals the appropriateness of its name. Pinto is a good producer of medium, white-fleshed potatoes, although it is not especially disease-resistant.

Kennebec

Pinto

Purple Viking

Russet Norkotah

Yellow Finn

Purple Viking

If ever a potato could be described as flashy, this is the one. Purple Viking sports rich violet skin streaked with bright salmon pink that overlays a very white and fine-textured flesh. Resistant to drought and scab, this all-purpose variety produces a hefty clump of medium and large potatoes.

Russet Norkotah

Russet Norkotah is a thick-skinned russet that bakes to perfection. A 1987 release from North Dakota, it produces a large amount of uniformly shaped tubers that mature fairly early for a russet. This variety stores well and is scab-resistant, although it is susceptible to verticillium wilt, early blight, and late blight.

Yellow Finn

Yellow Finn is fast becoming as popular as Yukon Gold. This Finnish potato also offers flavorful, buttery-yellow flesh, but Yukon Gold's tubers are more uniformly shaped than Yellow Finn's, which are flatter and can be somewhat irregular. These delicious potatoes are good keepers and have moderate resistance to scab.

LATE POTATOES (MORE THAN 90 DAYS)

Like midseason potatoes, late potatoes are planted mainly as storage potatoes and are often referred to in catalogs as a "main crop." In short-season areas, these should be planted at the same time as early varieties.

Bintje

Bintje, pronouced "bintchee," is a Dutch variety that dates back to 1911. It is known for its high yields of medium, luscious yellow potatoes. Because this variety sets so many tubers, a generous spacing of 15 in. to 18 in. is recommended when planting. Bintje stores moderately well and is drought-tolerant, but it is slightly susceptible to scab.

Butte

Butte is a long, shallow-eyed russet from Idaho, the state whose name is synonymous with baking potatoes. This high-yielding, fine-flavored variety is highly resistant to scab and late blight.

Bintje

Butte

Elba

Elba

Elba is a versatile, round, white all-purpose potato. Its slightly dry, waxy-textured flesh takes well to all methods of cooking. Elba is resistant to verticillium wilt, early blight, and late blight.

German Butterball

Among potato names, this one gets the award for "most enticing." It is a standout for flavor, yield, size, and vigor, producing large, smooth potatoes with slightly russetted skin. German Butterball is moderately resistant to scab.

German Butterball

Green Mountain

This Vermont variety was released in 1885 and has remained a favorite of gardeners because of its great flavor, which is retained over a long storage period. Its mealy-textured white flesh makes it a popular baking potato in New England. Green Mountain has resistance to fusarium and verticillium wilt but is susceptible to a number of viruses, scab, and late blight.

Green Mountain

Mainstay

Pimpernel

Red Pontiac

Mainstay
Mainstay is a new storage variety developed in Maine. It produces a respectable yield of round, smooth-skinned, all-purpose potatoes and is resistant to verticillium wilt and early blight.

Pimpernel
Pimpernel, for those unfamiliar with European wildflowers or an early 20th-century novel of swashbuckling and derring-do, refers to the Scarlet Pimpernel, a wayside plant with small red flowers. Of European origin, Pimpernel has red skin and golden flesh and makes a dandy baked potato. It also stores well and is tolerant of sandy soils and drought.

Red Pontiac
Red Pontiac is an old favorite all-purpose potato known for its great yields and fine flavor. This variety tends to produce large potatoes, and in the words of Maine grower Gene Frey, "Unless you're raising fodder for your spud cannon, plant closely to avoid oversized tubers, which can become knobby with second

Siberian

Banana

growth." Red Pontiac stores well and has some drought tolerance, although it is susceptible to scab.

Siberian

Siberian is a beauty, an heirloom variety featuring smooth, delicate ivory skin with magenta eyes and overlaid with rose-pink streaks. It is known for exceptional flavor and keeping qualities—and for vines that just don't quit, staying green until frost. Siberian, also known as Indian Pit, appears to have some resistance to scab.

FINGERLINGS

Fingerlings are the spuds to have when you're having more than one. These mid- to late-maturing potatoes are as small as 1½ in. but can grow to 6 in. Many do resemble fingers—rather bizarre fingers but nevertheless well within the bounds of a fruitful imagination. Their eating qualities are superb: they have irresistibly dense, buttery flesh with loads of flavor. If you've never thought that you could be happy eating a potato dosed only with salt and pepper, try a yellow-fleshed fingerling.

With their firm and waxy flesh, these little potatoes are excellent candidates for roasting, boiling, steaming, and in salads. Fans of fingerlings think that they also make a great baked potato.

Gardeners can count on fingerlings to make up for their small size with great productivity. Under optimum conditions, 1 pound of seed potatoes can produce 30 pounds of potatoes, but the average yield is 10 pounds. They are generally very scab resistant.

Banana

Banana is also known as Russian Banana. It is an easily grown, disease-resistant variety and has exceptionally high yields of luscious yellow-fleshed tubers. The banana tag comes from the shape, not the taste, of these tubers. This cultivar originated in the Baltic area and is probably the most familiar of the fingerlings.

French Fingerling

French Fingerling is a real beauty with deep rose-red skin and melt-in-your-mouth golden flesh. This variety produces good yields of uni-

French Fingerling

Ozette

formly shaped, medium-to-large, plump, waxy tubers and is the favorite fingerling of a number of growers. French Fingerling is also known as "Nosebag," a name attached to it because it is believed to have been first brought to this country in a horse's feedbag.

Ozette

All fingerlings are considered heirloom varieties, but Ozette, with its deep and numerous eyes encircling its stubby finger shape, has such a proto-potato appearance that it is easy to imagine it being harvested several thousand years ago in the high Andes. The name of this variety has been traced to a Makah Indian village near the farthest tip of Washington's Olympic peninsula. Ozette has been grown by generations of Makahs and is believed to have been brought from Peru in the late 1700s by Spanish explorers who traded with the tribe.

This fingerling has delicious ivory-colored flesh covered with thin tan skin. If you tend to peel potatoes, forget it with this one. Paring its numerous and deep eyes could delay dinner indefinitely; it's best to enjoy the superb taste, skins and all. Ozette plants are remarkably disease-resistant.

Peruvian Purple

Stunning deep amethyst-purple skin and lavender flesh make the Peruvian Purple a memorable potato. This medium, oblong-shaped potato is the mealiest of the fingerlings and provides a great-tasting combination of baked potato and conversation piece. Presprouting and planting early are recommended for northern gardens; Peruvian Purple needs a long season. It is one of the best storage potatoes.

Rose Finn Apple

This flavorsome little beauty has smooth rosy-buff skin and golden yellow flesh. The variety can give very large yields if it has good soil and a steady supply of moisture.

With the name Rose Finn Apple now attached to certified seed potatoes originating in a laboratory, the name confusion regarding this heir-

Peruvian Purple

Rose Finn Apple

loom variety may diminish. It is sometimes spelled Rose Fin Apple with the explanation that this cultivar sometimes produces odd, fin-shaped appendages.

Another alias is Rose Fir Apple. I have heard two stories attached to this name. The first is that this potato was always planted between rose bushes and fir trees, a highly unusual garden arrangement that suggests shade-grown potatoes. The second is that "fir apple" is the literal translation of a German word for pinecone, an image suggested by the potato's shape.

Swedish Peanut

This fancifully named variety produces appealing 2-in. to 4-in. taters that are shaped more like teardrops than peanuts. Mandel and Almond are other aliases. This potato has buff skin and yellow flesh, and like other fingerlings, it is a late variety with exceptional taste and texture. Swedish Peanut is particularly delicious roasted.

Swedish Peanut

Growing and Harvesting

A sampling of potatoes available to the home gardener.

Year by year, an elderly neighbor has reduced the size and variety of his vegetable garden to keep pace with his own reduced abilities. By now, he's down to rock-bottom basics—tomatoes, corn, and potatoes with a row of brilliant green lettuce in the spring. We all know that the best tomatoes, or "real tomatoes" as they're known around here, are homegrown. And we know that the finest corn on the cob is picked just as the pot of water starts to simmer, but potatoes? Why bother growing them when you can pick them up cheaply any time of year at the supermarket?

Well, more taste and more varieties for starters. You probably can't buy a 10-pound bag of French Fingerlings with glistening rose-red skin, rich yellow flesh, and exquisite flavor at your supermarket, but you can dig these potatoes from your backyard. For home gardeners, there are an astonishing number of varieties to be had through the mail. The fourth edition (1995) of the *Garden Seed Inventory* lists more than 200 commercially available varieties. They range in size from cherries to 1-pound lunkers, and the assortment of interior and exterior colors goes far beyond the standard white-fleshed supermarket varieties.

Another gratification of growing your own potatoes is the intense pleasure and excitement of the harvest. No harvesting satisfaction equals that of bringing in the taters. All summer they have been invisible in the secrecy and darkness of their underground chambers, engaged in transforming themselves from tiny, berry-sized spudlets into the real thing—the mature adult potato that you have been patiently awaiting. One fine fall day, you plunge your gardening fork under a pile of dessicated leaves and heave up a clutch of promising earthy lumps. At this moment, the phrase "earth apples" always comes to mind, the translation of the French name for potatoes, *"pommes de terres."* Year after year, I harvest potatoes and yet, with each harvest, I find myself surprised and gratified anew.

HOW MUCH SEED TO ORDER?

Since potato yields depend on soil, moisture, and variety, predicting harvest amounts is not an exact science. Following are some estimates that can help you figure out how many seed potatoes you need and how much they will yield.

Common Potatoes

1 pound of cut-up potatoes yields 8 to 10 seed pieces

1 pound of seed pieces plants 8 ft. to 10 ft. of a row at 12-in. spacing

1 pound of seed potatoes yields 10 pounds of potatoes

Fingerlings

1 pound of cut-up potatoes yields 20 seed pieces

1 pound of seed pieces plants 25 ft. to 30 ft. of a row at 15-in. to 18-in. spacing

1 pound of seed potatoes yields 20 pounds of potatoes

Minitubers

10 minitubers plant 10 ft. of a row at 12-in. spacing

1 minituber yields 2 to 3 pounds of potatoes

Potato plants occasionally produce seeds in a small, poisonous berry. Potatoes grown from seeds will be vastly different, giving potato breeders a chance to develop new varieties.

IN THE BEGINNING

When you plant potatoes, you engage in a little garden variety cloning. This is because the seed potatoes or minitubers that you plant are produced vegetatively and are genetically identical to their parents.

Seed potato is a term that refers to any potato stock set aside for the purpose of planting next season's crop. Since the early days of the domestication of the potato in the high fields of the Andes, putting aside seed potatoes has been the traditional method of propagation. Some catalogs now offer a high-tech alternative that has been christened minitubers. These are first-generation, marble-sized seed potatoes produced by tissue-cultured plants. These disease-free plants are propagated in a lab and raised under greenhouse conditions.

Since potatoes are such an important crop yet prone to many diseases, potato-growing states have seed certification programs to assure farmers and gardeners that their seed potatoes are disease-free. The process of certification begins when a grower enters minitubers produced by tissue-cultured plants into a state program. These minitubers are grown out in numbered lots and subjected to several greenhouse or field inspections by state agents. Each state has slightly different standards, but in general none allow more than 5% total disease in a seed lot. For seed certification, Maine requires a winter grow-out in Florida, where lot samples are further tested for disease and trueness to type.

Potato plants do occasionally produce seeds in a small, poisonous, green berry that results from blossom pollination. These seeds will produce a mixed bag of spuds. For plant breeders, this genetic diversity has potential for introducing new traits such as insect- and disease-resistance or improved flavor and texture.

DIVIDING TO MULTIPLY

"A potato the size of a small hen's egg" is a description that has been passed from grower to grower for generations as a rough guide as to whether a potato can be planted whole or must be divided up first. Potatoes fitting into the small hen's egg category may be planted as is, while larger ones should be cut into smaller pieces.

When you have larger potatoes, you should use a sharp knife to cut the potato into chunky blocks, each with two or three eyes and weighing 1 ounce to 4 ounces (1 ounce = 2 tablespoons, or 1 coffee scoop). The pieces should be cut with plenty of flesh around the eyes because the plant will utilize this stored energy during its first two to three weeks. Many varieties have eyes clustered at one end, so take care to distribute them evenly.

These sprouted potatoes have been cut into pieces suitable for planting.

For their small size, fingerlings produce an inordinate number of eyes. These eyes spiral the length of the tuber, so you may cut the potato into discs or wedges to end up with seed pieces with two or three eyes.

The number of eyes on a seed potato has a direct correlation to the number and size of potatoes you will get from it. One eye will produce a small crop of large tubers, while two eyes will produce some large ones along with some moderately sized spuds. Three eyes will produce more medium and small potatoes and fewer large ones.

To decrease the possibility of the seed potatoes rotting, it is a good idea to spread out the newly cut pieces and allow the cut surface to heal over, or suberize, for a day or two before planting.

Using supermarket potatoes as your seed potatoes is not recommended. Most have been treated with a sprout inhibitor, and commercial varieties may not be the best choice for home garden conditions.

PRESPROUTING

Presprouting, or "chitting" as it's called in England, is the practice of allowing seed potatoes to develop short sprouts before planting. This produces earlier potatoes, further helps to prevent rot, and may produce heavier yields.

About two weeks before planting, you should presprout your seed potatoes by spreading them with most of the eyes facing up in a single layer on a large horizontal surface or in stacking flats or boxes. The potatoes should then be exposed to medium light intensity in a warm (60° to 70°F) place. If your potatoes have been kept under cold conditions, bring them into a warm, dark place for two weeks to encourage sprouting, then expose them to light for two more weeks.

WHAT MAKES A POTATO HAPPY?

A healthy plant produces the most potatoes. To grow healthy plants, full sun and well-drained, fertile soil on the acidic side (a pH of 5.5 to 6.0 is ideal) are necessities. In building up your soil to this productive state, forego fresh manure, lime, and wood ash, as all of these will increase the incidence of scab, a superficial blemish that pits the skin of a potato. It is also wise to use restraint in high-nitrogen fertilizers, since too much nitrogen will cause a potato plant to put its energy into

Presprouting potatoes before planting gives the home gardener a head start.

leaves rather than into tubers. Recommended soil builders are compost and cover crops.

Potatoes prefer cool, moist weather. In the North, planting the early crop begins three to four weeks before the last frost. In the South, planting can begin as early as January. The soil temperature should be at least 45°F for early potatoes and 50°F for the main crop, and the soil must be dry enough to work, not wet and sticky. An old rule of thumb is to plant potatoes when the dandelions begin to bloom.

Consistent soil moisture is important during the growth cycle of potato plants, particularly during tuber formation when it will aid in preventing scab and misshapen potatoes.

For healthy plants, organic potato growers recommend foliar spraying with a fish emulsion and seaweed extract fertilizer. This should be applied early in the morning four to five times during the growing season.

PLANTING AND HILLING

When planting potatoes, keep in mind that the formation of new potatoes takes place above the seed piece. The traditional, and still the most common, growing method is to plant seed potatoes in trenches and hill them up as the plants grow.

To do this, begin by digging a shallow trench 4 in. to 6 in. deep and 3 in. wide. With the potato's eyes or sprouts facing upward, place seed pieces from common potatoes every 12 in. in the trench and those from fingerlings every 15 in. to 18 in. (Although small, fingerlings produce a large number of tubers per hill and need the extra room.) Cover the seed pieces with 2 in. to 4 in. of soil.

A constellation of potato blossoms illustrates their range of colors.

In approximately two weeks, depending on the soil temperature, you will see green leaves emerging from the soil. When these sprouts are about 6 in. high, gently form a hill around each group, leaving 2 in. to 3 in. of leaves exposed.

Hill a second time when the plants are 12 in. to 15 in. high. After this second hilling, the plants may be mulched to conserve moisture, keep the soil cool, and control weeds. Hilling is crucial to the formation of potatoes as it prevents the greening caused by exposure to light and gives the tubers room to develop.

In addition to the traditional trench, potatoes can also be planted in holes 4 in. to 6 in. deep.

Alternative growing methods

In addition to hilling, another way to grow potatoes is in vertical cylinders. This method produces a good deal of spuds in a small area and is a great solution for gardeners with limited space or poor soil. The vertical containers can be barrels or garbage cans with bottom drainage holes or wire cylinders 23 in. in diameter made of a 6-ft. length of 36-in.-wide chicken wire formed into a circle.

Begin by placing your growing containers 12 in. apart on soil that has been turned under.

Line the interiors of the wire cylinders with hay, compost, old straw, or grass clippings, then place the seed pieces 6 in. to 8 in. apart and cover with 2 in. to 4 in. of soil. When the leaves emerge and reach 6 in. high, add 4 in. of soil or organic mulching material. As the plant stems lengthen, so do the underground stolons that produce potatoes. Water requirements increase when growing within wire cylinders, so check the plants frequently in warm weather.

A third way to grow potatoes is under a layer of mulch, a method to consider if your soil is shallow, compacted, or contains scab-producing organisms. Growing under mulch produces an easy harvest of lovely, clean spuds, but the harvest will be smaller and may have a few mousebites taken out. A generous supply of mulch, which can be seed-free hay, straw, grass clippings, or leaves, is required. This method requires less space than conventional planting and hilling. Because no hilling is required and the dirt for hilling comes from wide rows, rows can be spaced closer together at 18 in. to 24 in. apart.

To use this method, prepare your planting area as usual. Seed pieces may be placed directly on the ground or in a 4-in.-deep depression or trench. Loosely shake mulch over the rows to a height of 6 in. to 10 in. As the leaves emerge and the plants grow, continue to add mulch, as if hilling. Be sure that the tubers are well covered and kept in the dark.

AN OUNCE OF PREVENTION

Potatoes are prone to a host of disease and insect problems that can be mitigated by preventive measures. Some of these measures, such as annual additions of organic material to the soil to create a rich, loose growing medium, are standard practices followed by careful gardeners. Another important practice is a four-year crop rotation. Since potatoes are members of the *Solanaceae* family, they should not follow their tomato, pepper, or eggplant relatives in a particular plot of soil. Diseased plants should be removed from the garden, and after harvest, withered potato plants should be gathered up and thoroughly composted in a hot compost pile or disposed of to prevent the spread of any residual diseases. (See the sidebar on p. 38 on some common diseases.)

The ubiquitous potato beetle is a complaint of many gardeners. One way to handle this pest is to deny it access to your plants by covering them with a lightweight spunbonded polypropylene designed specifically as an insect barrier. Keep an eye out for the emergence of the first potato beetles and immediately handpick and destroy them, then do the same with their yellow egg masses on leaf undersides and their destructive yellow larvae. If the numbers are beyond handpicking, you can use the biological pest control *Bacillus thuringiensis*, better known as Bt. The specific variety "san diego" kills early stages of the larvae.

HARVESTING

The classic potato harvest scene has the happy gardener setting out on a crisp fall morning, digging fork in hand, and whistling merrily in anticipation of uncovering the longed-for buried treasure. But you don't have to wait that long; the harvest can begin with new potatoes.

Growing potatoes under mulch requires less space than the conventional method of trenching then hilling with soil.

POTATO PROBLEMS

Potatoes are subject to a number of diseases and pests. Here are the most common.

Early Blight

Early blight occurs in wet weather. Although it infects young leaf tissue during moist conditions, the ½-in. brown lesions do not develop until the foliage ages or is stressed. These lesions are made up of dark brown concentric rings that resemble a target. During harvest, spores from the foliage may infect tubers, which will then develop brown or black sunken spots in storage.

Late Blight

Late blight is a serious disease when cool, damp weather occurs regularly during the potato season. Leaf lesions are brown to purplish black with pale green or yellow margins.

During humid or wet weather, a halo of whitish, downy mildew may appear around these lesions. On tubers, a reddish-brown dry rot turns the potato soft and destroys it.

Scab

Scab, which looks exactly like its name, is strictly a surface blemish. These corky lesions occur when soil moisture is low during initial tuber formation. It is most likely to occur in soils with a pH higher than 5.2 and is also fostered by the use of fresh manure.

Verticillium Wilt

Verticillium wilt is one of the most widespread diseases of potatoes. It affects the water-conducting tissue (xylem) of the plant, causing it to turn reddish brown. This can be seen by slicing through the stems at an angle near the soil line. An early symptom of this condition is leaves turning yellow, then brown, resulting in the appearance of premature aging.

Leafhoppers

Leafhoppers are a problem in the East, where they cause "hopper burn," a foliage injury that results in premature aging and greatly reduces yield and quality. Leafhoppers feed on the undersurfaces of potato leaves, which causes a speckled appearance.

Potatoes blossom at the same time tuber formation begins. This is your signal that new potatoes may be ready and you can indulge in an age-old practice called "robbing." You can stick your hand into the side of a potato hill and poke around to discover what's inside, but do this gently to avoid injuring the remaining roots. You can rob several potatoes from several plants, or you can sacrifice an entire plant or two at the end of your row. If you develop a taste for retrieving these delicacies from your backyard, you can plant a row of early potatoes specifically for harvesting as new potatoes.

To store your potatoes, they should be mature and the foliage dead. Frost will kill the foliage but if there is no frost in sight, you can pull or cut it. The potatoes need to remain in the ground for 10 to 14 days to toughen the skin.

The ideal harvest day is sunny and dry. To dig your potatoes, plunge your digging fork in outside the hill to avoid spearing a perfectly good potato. Once the potatoes are dug out, allow them to air-dry for a couple of hours to further toughen the skin before gathering them up. Some gardeners prefer to store their potatoes

For home gardeners, harvesting new potatoes is an eagerly awaited event.

A splendid harvest of hosed-off potatoes dries out-doors before being sorted and stored.

unwashed, but I like to hose mine off on the lawn. When they are dry, I then proceed to the sorting.

Before storing your crop, it is important to sort your potatoes. The first pile to make is of all those damaged in any way in the harvest. These should be eaten first. Next, I like to group the baking potatoes together. With the remainders, I separate the great keepers from the merely good keepers. My yellow-fleshed and fingerling varieties also get their own box.

If you are saving seed potatoes for next year's crop, now is the time to put them aside. Pick medium-sized samples typical of the variety that are completely free of blemishes, wounds, and soft spots. Put them in paper bags labeled with the variety's name, and store them under conditions that are as ideal as possible (see pp. 44-45).

Buying
and Storing

Until recently, buying potatoes in a supermarket did not take much thought. Reach down, grab a bag, haul 'em into the cart, and try to remember what else was on the grocery list that you left on the kitchen table. Now, however, we've got some interesting choices to make. Tiny new red potatoes from Florida? Yukon Golds with their buttery-yellow flesh? What about those purple-skinned ones that are lavender on the inside? Or those lumpy and appealing little fingerlings?

The types of potatoes available to us in supermarkets has changed, but one of their most important characteristics has remained a constant: their exceptional keeping qualities. Although potatoes are excellent keepers, during storage they are merely dormant; the irresistable urge to sprout and regenerate is slowed but will come out eventually. Because of this time limit on effective storage, the year-round availability of potatoes is due mainly to staggered harvesting all over the country. For example, on the East Coast, the harvest of tiny new red potatoes begins in March in Florida. As the season progresses, the harvest moves up the coast to the Carolinas and Virginia and ends with Maine, Nova Scotia, and Prince Edward Island.

POTATO TYPES
In most supermarkets, produce managers traditionally categorize potatoes not by variety but by appearance. This has led to four basic types.

In supermarkets, produce managers categorize most potatoes as russets, long whites, round reds, and round whites.

California russets begin to arrive in the markets in August and September; those from Idaho later in the fall.

Long Whites
Long whites are characterized by their elliptical shape and very thin, almost translucent, smooth, tan skin. Most of these all-purpose potatoes begin to arrive from California in May and June.

Round Reds
These are not always round (some are oblong), but they are always red, although rose or deep pink might be a more accurate color description. Because of their low starch content, these boiling, or waxy, potatoes are the ones to buy for salads or any dish that requires potatoes that hold their shape.

Round Whites
White flesh, tan skin, and a rounded shape characterize these all-purpose potatoes.

Other Potato Categories
In addition to the four basic commercial types, there is a catchall category of "Specials" or "Novelties." Yukon Golds, fingerlings, blue- or red-fleshed potatoes, and Peewees, which are small, thumb-sized potatoes popular for boiling, all come under this heading.

"Creamer" is another term that you may see in your supermarket's potato display. This name refers to potatoes that are 1 in. or less in diameter. They may be new potatoes or they may be fully matured tiny ones.

Although most people think of new potatoes as small red ones, the term "new" refers to any freshly harvested, immature potato of any variety. They are shipped from Florida in March and continue to be harvested from California,

Although typically associated with red-skinned varieties, new potatoes are any type of freshly harvested, immature potato.

Russets
Also called Idaho potatoes (no matter where they're from), these lengthy, leathery-skinned ovals are the quintessential baking potato. Their high starch content also means they make the best mashed and french-fried potatoes.

the Carolinas, Virginia, the Midwest, and the Northwest as the season progresses.

New potatoes have thinner skins and slightly moister flesh than more mature varieties; it is their thin and tender skin that is their hallmark. Don't be fooled by red potatoes being marketed as "new" potatoes during the fall and winter. The late date, as well as the thicker skins, will tell you that these are mature round reds.

New potatoes are perishable, so you should use them within a week or store them in the vegetable crisper of your refrigerator. They are at their best steamed, boiled, roasted, or in salads.

WHAT TO LOOK FOR

The potatoes that you want to take home with you should be smooth-skinned, show no evidence of sprouts, and be free of cuts, bruises, and dark spots. They should feel heavy in the hand and have no visible greenish tint to the skin (see the sidebar below).

GREEN MEANS CAUTION

The green that may appear on potatoes when they are exposed to light is chlorophyll. The chlorophyll itself is not dangerous, but it is evidence that solanine, an alkaloid found in the leaves of tomatoes, eggplants, and peppers, is present. Small amounts of solanine are normal in a potato and contribute to its flavor. However, when a potato is bruised, exposed to light, or is sprouting, additional amounts are produced, concentrating in the potato's eyes and skin.

To be harmed by solanine, you would have to eat 2½ pounds of cooked green potatoes. After this spud-eating binge, the onset of headache, diarrhea, and nausea would alert you to solanine poisoning. Potatoes that produce a burning, peppery sensation on the tongue are also suspect, as this indicates high levels of alkaloids.

Finding a few green potatoes is certainly no reason to throw out your supply. Since solanine is concentrated in the skin, peeling your potatoes to a depth of 1/16 in. and removing the sprouts make them safe to eat.

A greenish tinge on a potato actually comes from chlorophyll but indicates a possibly harmful amount of a toxic alkaloid, solanine. Since solanine is concentrated in the skin, peeling potatoes to a depth of 1/16 in. and removing any sprouts will make them safe to eat.

Potatoes left in storage too long take on a life of their own.

Potatoes can be purchased loose or packaged, usually in 5- or 10-pound bags. The larger amounts in bags are usually cheaper but will be no bargain if you don't have a dark and cool storage area.

SHORT-TERM STORAGE
With potatoes available year-round from supermarkets, the need for long-term storage in the home has diminished. Most cooks know that it is imperative to keep potatoes in the dark to prevent greening. This condition is easily met in the average kitchen cabinet, but the kitchen cabinet usually lacks the low temperatures and high humidity required for ideal potato storage.

Cool air is important in storing potatoes. At 45° to 50°F, they should keep well for about a month. Warmer temperatures encourage sprouting and shriveling.

Potatoes can be stored in the dark and humid atmosphere of the vegetable crisper in a refrigerator. However, a note of caution: potatoes held at 35°F or lower convert their starch to sugars, resulting in a strange, sweet taste. Keeping them at room temperature for several days will reverse the process and restore the starch. If potatoes freeze, they are ruined.

LONG-TERM STORAGE
The fact that potatoes could be stored throughout the winter, when very little other food was available, has accounted for their importance

since they were first domesticated in the Andes thousands of years ago. Under the right conditions, potatoes can be kept in good shape for four to six months. These conditions are complete darkness, high humidity (80% to 90%) and low temperatures (36° to 45°F).

This combination of darkness, humidity, and cold exists in a good root cellar, a cold-storage area that used to be built into farmhouse basements. Without a root cellar, or even an old farmhouse with its inevitable cold spots, ingenuity is called for.

If you have a space such as a partially heated garage or an unheated closet or enclosed porch, long-term storage of mature potatoes is possible, as long as the temperature remains above 35°F. The first step is always to inspect potatoes for bruises, cuts, and soft or open spots. You should use any that exhibit these blemishes right away; they won't store well. Pack those that pass muster in paper bags, wooden or plastic crates, or cardboard cartons. Because potatoes differ in the length of time they will remain in good condition, store different varieties separately. If light is a problem, place the potatoes in a cardboard carton and pile newspapers on top to block the light.

Potato hoarders living in an old house with a cellar entrance protected by a sloping bulkhead can use the space between the bulkhead and the cellar door for cold storage. Insulate the bulkhead with rigid foam insulation and use the steps as shelves. On exceptionally cold days, open the inner cellar door to regulate the temperature and prevent freezing.

Experts recommend that potatoes be stored separately from apples. Apples give off ethylene gas, which promotes ripening and, in the case of potatoes, sprouting. However, it's not always

A dark, cool, and humid root cellar provides ideal storage conditions for potatoes.

practical to segregate the two. Potato grower David Ronniger has found that ventilation is the solution. In a well-ventilated root cellar, the ethylene gas will be carried off by air currents instead of settling around the stored produce. (For more detailed information on long-term produce storage, I recommend *Root Cellaring* by Mike and Nancy Bubel, published by Storey Communications in 1991.)

Cooking

Of all vegetables, potatoes may be the most evocative. They are elemental and emotional, often strongly connected to memories. A search of my own potato image bank brings up dinner at Uncle Joe's.

Uncle Joe, formerly an important and powerful man, was in his dotage when I was a child. He had retained his wealth but lost his hearing and was enfeebled and confused by arteriosclerosis. He had never married. Once a month, my parents, two sisters, and I would pile into our used car, leave our Virginia suburb, and appear at Uncle Joe's three-story brick residence in Washington, D.C., for a formal Sunday dinner where we were invariably the only guests. Because of my great-uncle's deafness, dinner conversation around his massive mahogany table consisted of shouted remarks or questions directed his way. These loud bursts were interspersed with remarks quietly muttered among my own family for the sole purpose of producing an involuntary crack in someone's politely composed facade.

The main course was often roast beef, cooked to perfection by Uncle Joe's ancient and faithful Irish cook, Mary. Although roast beef was at the top of our "favorite foods we never get at home" list, what made this offering even more mouthwatering was the circlet of peeled and roasted potatoes surrounding it. Brown and golden, these ordinary vegetables were transformed by fire and fat into food of the gods. They were dense, tender, succulent wholes encased in a toasty brown wrapping that carried the essence of roasted meat. Forty years later, my family still rhapsodizes about Mary's potatoes.

POTATO YIELDS

Here are some helpful rules of thumb to use as guidelines when you don't have a recipe or if your recipe calls for pounds of potatoes.

1 medium potato = 1 serving

3 medium potatoes = 1 pound

1 pound = 3 cups of sliced potatoes

1 pound = 2½ cups of diced potatoes

1 pound = 2 cups of mashed potatoes

1 pound = 3 servings of potato salad

2 large baking potatoes = 1½ pounds

4 large baking potatoes (3 pounds), baked and mashed = 6 cups

4 small, 1-in. to 1½-in. new potatoes = 1 serving

10 to 12 new potatoes = 1 pound

When planning amounts of mashed potatoes, a handy rule of thumb to remember is that 1 pound, or 3 medium potatoes, produces about 2 cups of mashed potatoes.

HIGH OR LOW STARCH?

If you are uncertain about the starch content of your stored potatoes and are making a dish where starch content is critical, such as potato salad, here are two methods to determine the amount of starch. The most reliable method is to make a brine of 1 part salt to 11 parts water and place the potato in it. A low-starch boiling potato will float, while a high-starch potato, being denser, will sink. Another method is to cut a potato in half: if it sticks to the knife or if a filmy or foamy residue is left on the knife, the potato has a high starch content.

Three different potatoes, three different amounts of starch. Using the right potato means the difference between a salad or gratin with distinct slices or one that is only a few steps removed from mashed potatoes.

Mary's potatoes are an example of why this vegetable remains a kitchen favorite. Its form and texture lend the potato to a number of basic cooking methods, and with its amenable neutrality, it can easily be coaxed into an inspiring and memorable dish.

THE EFFECTS OF STARCH CONTENT

If you've ever wondered why your potato salad is only steps away from mashed potatoes, the answer lies in the starch content. Starch content affects the cooking properties of potatoes more than any other factor, and knowing about it can help to unravel the mystery of how a particular variety will perform with various cooking methods.

A potato is the swollen tip of an underground stem where the potato plant stores energy in the form of starch. The purpose of this starch is to support the new growth from the eyes, which will result in new plants. Starch is measured by specific gravity readings that compare the density of a potato variety with the density of water. Very dense potatoes are high in starch; those less dense are correspondingly lower in starch.

High-starch potatoes, often termed bakers, have a drier and mealier texture than low-starch ones and are best for baking, mashing, and french fries. When boiled or steamed, they absorb water and tend to crumble. This is because the cells of a high-starch potato separate when cooked. All russet potatoes (so called for the netted texture, or russeting, of their skin) fall into this category. Butte, Burbank, Russet Norkotah, and Sierra are some of the most common commercial russet varieties.

Low-starch types, such as most fingerlings and red-skinned potatoes, have firm, moist textures and maintain their shapes when cooked. They are termed boiling, or waxy, potatoes and are best for dishes where it is important that slices or pieces of cut potato remain intact: salads, sautés, stews, and au gratin dishes.

Between these two categories are all-purpose varieties with a medium amount of starch. Many of the older varieties, such as Kennebec, Katahdin, and Irish Cobbler, fall into this category. Commercially available long white types, such as White Rose, are medium-starch varieties, as are Yellow Finn and Yukon Gold.

All-purpose potatoes are versatile. They hold their shapes when boiled and are superb roasted or scalloped. They are also delicious baked, although they will not be as mealy and crisp-skinned as russets. Yukon Gold has become a personal favorite for creamy and buttery-looking mashed potatoes.

TO PEEL OR NOT TO PEEL

Once upon a time, whether or not to peel a potato was not a question that a cook would waste any time pondering. You peeled a spud and that was that.

But that was before researchers started looking into potato skins. They discovered that although the interior flesh of the potato accounts for most of the vitamins, in terms of the total weight of a potato the skin contains a disproportionate amount of nutrients. This is when mothers across the country began to urge their families to eat *all* of their baked potatoes.

In 1987, researchers at Cornell University created a national uproar when their work documented toxic glycoalkaloids in potato skins. They recommended peeling away ³⁄₁₆ in. before cooking to prevent the migration of these alkaloids from the skin to the interior. In response to a press release from Cornell, newspapers across the country printed stories with headlines such as "Warning: Peel Potatoes before Cooking" and "Remember Mom's Advice to Eat the Potato Skin? She Was Wrong."

This research has been criticized on the grounds that the number of samples used in the study was far too small to be taken seriously, that dose-response considerations were not mentioned, and that it was not new information. Scientists have known for decades that glycoalkaloids do have the potential to cause unpleasant symptoms (diarrhea, headaches, nausea) and in a few extreme cases, death. However, the majority of the vast amount of potatoes consumed every day around the world do not contain glycoalkaloids in high enough concentrations to pose any problems.

Production of glycoalkaloids in potatoes, especially in small or immature ones, is stimulated by exposure to light and by either very cold or warm storage. Fortunately, there are warning signs of these conditions. Exposure to light causes potatoes to produce chlorophyll, so green tubers are automatically suspect. Glycoalkaloids also produce a bitter, peppery sensation on the tongue. Since these substances are not destroyed by cooking and are concentrated on the surface and in the sprouts of the potato, always check for and peel away any green areas and remove all sprouts.

Another substance that may be found on the surface of potatoes is a chemical sprout inhibitor known as CIPC that is used in 90% to 95% of all stored potatoes. The Natural Resources Defense Council reports that there is some evidence of CIPC causing mutagenic effects in laboratory testing but that tests on its carcinogenic properties have not been sufficient.

The crux of the potato-peeling debate is that a peeled potato loses nutrients during cooking through its cut flesh. Vitamins C and B found in potatoes are water soluble and leach out

Boiled new potatoes are one of life's simple pleasures and reason enough to offer up thanks for this humble tuber.

into cooking water. Cooking unpeeled potatoes whole is the best way to conserve these nutrients.

This leaching of nutrients through the cut surface of a potato is why storing cut potatoes in cold water until they are cooked to prevent their darkening is no longer recommended. To preserve the color of cut potatoes, toss them with an ascorbic or citric acid mix or some lemon juice.

BOILING

If you are boiling potatoes to use in a dish where it's important that they retain their shapes, be sure to use a boiling or all-purpose type. To ensure even cooking, choose spuds of the same size. Begin by scrubbing them with water and a stiff brush or in the case of tender-skinned new potatoes, something softer such as a sponge. To boil potatoes, place them in a medium to large lidded pot and cover with water by 1 in. Cover and bring to a boil over high heat, then lower the heat and simmer until the largest potato is fork tender. The term "fork tender" may seem glaringly obvious. However, to avoid undercooked potatoes, use a table fork, not a knife, icepick, or even a large, two-pronged grilling fork, to test for doneness. For whole potatoes, cooking takes 30 to 45 minutes; cut-up potatoes take 15 to 20 minutes.

Preparing new potatoes

A boiled potato can be an end in itself or the beginning of a sublime dish. Like the first asparagus and peas, the appearance of summer's first new potatoes is a special event for both gardeners and consumers. Cover and boil these tender morsels 15 to 25 minutes, depending on their size, then drain and return them to the pot, gently rotating them over the heat to dry. Since the arrival of new potatoes is always a celebration, I like to indulge myself by rolling them around in melted butter and serving them topped with chopped fresh chives or dill, salt, and freshly ground black pepper. This is one of life's simple pleasures and reason enough to offer up profound thanks for this humble tuber.

Preparing home fries

Boiled potatoes are the beginning of home fries, a dish so important in American cuisine that it holds within its name two words that

• To save time in the oven, boil a baking potato for 10 minutes, then bake at 400°F for 30 minutes.

• If you're a fan of roasted garlic, roast an unpeeled head of garlic on a small square of aluminum foil along with your baking potatoes. Cut a cross into the top of the potato, squeeze in a couple of roasted garlic cloves, a little butter, and salt, and mix them into the potato flesh.

• To reheat a baked potato, dip it into water and rebake it in a preheated 350°F oven for 20 minutes.

• Use leftover baked potatoes to make great home fries.

• For simple and savory stuffed baked potatoes, slice off the top one-quarters of hot baked potatoes, and scoop all of the flesh into a bowl. Add cubes of low-fat Neufchatel cheese and a bit of adobo sauce in which canned chipotle chiles are packed, then mash until smooth. Season with salt and pepper, stuff into the potato skins, and reheat if necessary.

quiver with cultural resonance: "home" and "fries." When you are boiling potatoes for a specific recipe, future home fries are a reason to boil extra. Prepare this dish by slicing or cubing leftover boiled (or steamed) potatoes and chopping a little onion. Brown the potatoes and onions in a small amount of butter in a nonstick or cast-iron frying pan, then season with salt and freshly ground black pepper. Taste a forkful and you've got a good idea of why potatoes are regarded as comfort food.

BAKING

Waverley Root, the great food writer, asked his French wife what her favorite American food was after her first visit to this country. "Idaho baked potatoes," she replied. Baked potatoes are a very American food and a very fine one at that. But not all baking potatoes originate in Idaho, in spite of the aims of the Idaho Potato Council. Any potato is delicious baked, but the best baked potatoes come from high-starch types such as russets, most of which are grown commercially in Idaho and California. High-

Another of life's simple pleasures is a hot baked potato, crisp on the outside, dry and mealy on the inside.

starch types produce delectably dry and crumbly flesh when baked.

To bake potatoes, preheat the oven to 400° to 450°F. Gently scrub the potatoes under running water and pat dry. With a fork, pierce the potato skin in several places to allow steam to escape. Place the potatoes directly on the oven rack, leaving 1 in. to 2 in. between each potato and any other dish that may be sharing the oven. Depending on the potato size and what else is in the oven, bake between 45 minutes and 1¼ hours. (Potatoes may be baked at a lower temperature to accompany a roast or casserole but will take a proportionately longer time to cook.) To test for doneness, hold the largest potato in a potholder and squeeze it to feel if it is soft enough or test it with the prongs of a table fork. The longer you bake it, the softer the center and crispier the skin.

To serve, cut a cross in the top of the potato and squeeze from the bottom to push up the flesh. The classic toppings for baked potatoes are butter or sour cream with judicious amounts of salt and pepper. (For other toppings, see pp. 116-117.)

A sampling of low-tech methods for making fluffy and delicious mashed potatoes (clockwise from top): food mill, ricer, potato masher, and another type of ricer.

STEAMING

Steaming a potato is the best method to preserve its shape and texture and can add flavor when an aromatic steaming liquid is used.

To use this method, place a steamer basket in a lidded pan and add water to just below the bottom of the basket. Over high heat, bring the water to a boil, then lower the heat to a simmer, add whole or cut-up boiling or all-purpose potatoes, and cover. Steam until tender, 15 to 45 minutes, depending on the size and amount of potatoes. Be sure to check the water level occasionally to see that it hasn't boiled away.

For a subtle infusion of flavor, you can add aromatic ingredients to the steaming liquid. Lemon, garlic, and rosemary make an especially flavorsome combination, while others to try are fresh ginger root, dried and fresh herbs, Dijon mustard, garlic-chile paste, and citrus peels.

MASHING

Mashed potatoes, like the gravy often ladled over them, can be the subject of contention. Perhaps this is because they have become a staple in holiday or festive meals, a fluffy mound of white to provide a catch basin for gravy from the celebratory roast. Holidays are occasions that bring families together, and family dishes are dependably traditional. Feelings can run high if a favorite dish is altered, so there have come to be a number of squabbling factions in the Mashed Potato League. One cook will swear that mashing potatoes with an electric mixer makes them gluey and will use only a potato masher or ricer (see the sidebar on the facing page). Another will use only a silver fork, while a third adds only the cooking liquid, never milk or cream.

CLASSIC MASHED POTATOES

Whether to use an electric mixer or a potato ricer or masher when making mashed potatoes is a matter of preference. They do produce different textures: an electric mixer makes a stickier, creamier mash, while a potato ricer or masher gives a lighter, mealier result.

For any one of these methods, begin by boiling or steaming six potatoes until thoroughly cooked. If you are using a potato ricer, drain, cut up, and transfer the potatoes to the ricer. Press into a heated bowl, then beating with a whisk or fork, add ½ cup warm milk and 2 tablespoons softened or cut-up butter.

If you are using a potato masher, drain and peel the potatoes and transfer them to a large heated bowl. Using an up-and-down motion to incorporate as much air as possible, mash the potatoes until fluffy, adding ½ cup warmed milk and 2 tablespoons softened or cut-up butter.

If you are using an electric mixer, drain and peel the potatoes and transfer them to a large heated

With a ricer, it is not necessary to peel potatoes. The peels from the cut-up chunks are retained in the ricer and can be easily removed.

bowl. Using the mixer on a moderate speed, purée the potatoes with 2 tablespoons butter. Add milk gradually until the desired consistency is reached; less may be needed than with the previous methods. Season with salt. These mashed potatoes serve 6.

Utensils and ingredients may be a matter of opinion, but here are some facts about mashed potatoes.

• Because of their high starch content, baking potatoes make the lightest and fluffiest mashed potatoes.

• Potatoes must be thoroughly cooked; undercooked potatoes will not mash properly.

• Potatoes must be mashed while hot and are best served at once. Once cooled, a cooked potato will never regain its mealiness.

• With a potato ricer, it is not necessary to peel potatoes. The peels are retained in the ricer and are easily removed.

• Mashed potatoes are best served immediately in a heated dish. If this is not possible, they may be kept hot in a partially covered container over hot water. (They need air circulation so they don't develop an off taste.) Fluff before serving.

Potatoes roasted with carrots, beets, parsnips, celeriac, and onions make a satisfying autumn or winter dish.

ROASTING

Pan-roasting potatoes is one of the easiest and most delicious ways of preparing these noble tubers. The traditional method of roasting them has been to cook them along with meat. However, with the Sunday roast having gone the way of Jello molds, roasted potatoes have come into their own. Anointed with oil or butter and sprinkled with savory herbs such as chopped fresh rosemary or dill or mixed with paper-thin slices of garlic, potatoes develop a crisp, browned exterior and a soft and succu-

lent interior. When they are roasted with carrots, beets, parsnips, celeriac, and onions, a delectable mélange results, one that makes a fine autumn entrée.

To roast potatoes, preheat the oven to 400°F. Peel and cut the potatoes into wedges or chunks, then arrange them in a single layer in a shallow pan and toss with oil or melted butter, salt, and freshly ground black pepper. Bake for 45 minutes, or until fork tender, turning occasionally with a spatula.

To roast potatoes with meat, arrange small or halved peeled potatoes around the meat about 1½ hours before serving. Brush or baste the potatoes with the pan drippings, making sure to turn and baste them frequently so they will brown. My great-uncle's Irish cook always said the secret of her irresistible potatoes was that when she took the roast out of the oven, she turned the temperature up to 450°F and finished the potatoes with additional browning from this high heat.

GRILLING

The advances in grilling design and technology over the last decade as well as the culinary waves that emanate from California have popularized both outdoor and indoor grilling. Potatoes take to grilling like a duck takes to water.

Thin slices or wedges can be cooked directly over coals (see Grilled Rosemary and Garlic Potatoes on p. 110), but for heftier chunks, such as those used in shish kebabs, parboiling potatoes saves time and ensures thorough cooking. To parboil, simmer large potatoes 10 to 12 minutes, or until they are barely tender when pricked with a fork. Cut the potatoes into the appropriate shapes for your recipe, and toss with flavored oil or melted butter to prevent them from drying out.

Another method for cooking potatoes on the grill is to cook them in a packet of heavy-duty aluminum foil. This results in potatoes that are caramelized and crusty where they touch the foil. To use this method, place thinly sliced boiling or all-purpose potatoes in the center of a large piece of foil. Add butter or olive oil, salt, black pepper, and the flavorings of your choice. Garlic is always good, and you can add a bit of lime juice, cilantro, and cumin for a Mexican slant. The simple combination of tarragon and butter is also divine. Next, fold the foil to form a tightly sealed pouch and place it on the grill. Cook 30 to 40 minutes, turning every 10 minutes.

MICROWAVING

Friends who have microwave ovens extol two characteristics of microwaving: it's great for reheating leftovers, and you can have baked potatoes in 8 minutes. To bake potatoes in a microwave oven, start by choosing spuds of the same size. Scrub, pat dry, and prick the potatoes in several places with a fork. Next, place the potatoes on a double layer of paper towels with one in the middle and the rest arranged like spokes with the small end pointing inward. For cooking times, consult the microwave's manual because they differ from model to model. Turn the potatoes over halfway through the cooking cycle. Before testing for doneness, allow the potatoes to rest for 5 minutes since they continue to cook after removal from the microwave. The skin of microwave baked potatoes can be crisped by placing them in a preheated 400°F oven for 10 minutes.

Microwaving is also a good way to preserve the colored flesh of certain blue potatoes, whose hue is sometimes diminished by longer and moister cooking methods.

DEEP-FRYING

Homemade french-fried potatoes are out of this world but a heap of trouble to prepare. Should you have an uncontrollable urge to experience life in the 1950s when a deep fryer was considered a kitchen necessity, here, from The Potato Board, is how to make french fries.

Peel russet potatoes and cut them into strips about ¼ in. thick. As you're cutting, toss the strips into a bowl of ice water to keep them crisp and white. (They should remain in the ice water for as short a time as possible to prevent water absorption, which prolongs the cooking time and makes the potatoes oily and soggy.)

Pat the strips dry with paper towels and heat about 4 in. of vegetable or peanut oil to 390°F in a deep fryer or large heavy saucepan. Place a layer of potato strips in a wire basket and immerse the basket in the hot oil, or place the strips, a few at a time, directly into the oil. Cook about 5 minutes, or until the strips are golden brown and tender. Remove the strips from the oil, drain well on paper towels, then salt lightly and serve immediately or keep warm in a 300°F oven.

Recipes

Appetizers

Potato and Carrot Ajlouke
(recipe on page 60)

POTATO AND CARROT AJLOUKE

2 cups water

2 strips orange peel, 2 inches to 3 inches long

2 cloves garlic, bruised and cut in half lengthwise

1 cinnamon stick, broken, or ¼ teaspoon ground cinnamon

1 large potato, peeled and cut into 1-inch chunks

2 large carrots, peeled and cut into 1-inch chunks

2 tablespoons freshly squeezed lemon juice

1 tablespoon minced cilantro

½ teaspoon caraway seeds, ground

½ teaspoon ground coriander seeds

pinch of ground red pepper

salt, to taste

This easy, nonfat dip comes from North Africa. Its main ingredients are steamed over an aromatic liquid that imparts subtle flavoring and fills the kitchen with a marvelous fragrance. Crisp raw vegetables or triangles of toasted pita bread complement the dip's spiciness and lovely pale-orange color. (Photo on page 58.)

Pour the water into the bottom of a steaming pan. Add the orange peel, garlic, and cinnamon, bring to a boil, then lower the heat to a simmer. Place the potatoes and carrots in the steamer basket, then put the basket in the pan. Cover and steam 25 minutes, or until the vegetables are tender. (Check the water level occasionally to determine if more should be added.)

Cool slightly and transfer the potatoes and carrots to a potato ricer or medium bowl. Rice or mash to a coarse purée. Stir in the lemon juice, cilantro, caraway, coriander, and red pepper. Season with salt. Serve at room temperature.

Yields 1½ cups

SKORDALIA

2 large Yukon Gold or russet
   potatoes
½ cup low-fat plain yogurt
2 cloves garlic, minced
¼ cup chopped fresh parsley
¼ cup toasted almonds,
   ground
½ teaspoon dried red pepper
   flakes
2 tablespoons lemon juice
1 tablespoon extra-virgin
   olive oil
salt and freshly ground black
   pepper, to taste

Skorda is Greek for garlic, and skordalia is a dip or sauce made with a base of cooked, mashed potato and flavored with garlic. The other ingredients vary from cook to cook. This recipe makes a luscious dip that quickly disappears when served with an assortment of colorful, fresh, raw vegetables cut into bite-sized portions and arranged on a platter. You could also serve this with triangles of toasted pita bread. Thinned with water or broth, this sauce can be used for fish, poultry, or cooked vegetables.

Boil the potatoes 35-40 minutes, or until tender. Allow them to cool slightly, then peel. In a medium bowl, rice or thoroughly mash the potatoes and combine with the yogurt. Stir in the garlic, parsley, almonds, red pepper, lemon juice, and olive oil. Season with salt and pepper. Serve at room temperature.

Yields 2¼ cups

TINY NEW POTATOES
WITH A FRESH HERB DIP

24-28 tiny new potatoes,
    1 inch to 1½ inches in
    diameter

Dip
½ cup low-fat sour cream
½ cup low-fat plain yogurt
2 tablespoons minced chives
1 teaspoon minced fresh
    thyme
salt and freshly ground black
    pepper, to taste

The appearance of these tender miniatures in the market or garden is an eagerly anticipated event, a cause for celebration. The best treatment of new potatoes is a simple and direct one. This recipe will please the cook with its ease and please guests with its combination of herb-flavored creaminess and thin-skinned, delicate new potatoes.

In a large pot, cover the potatoes with water and bring to a boil over high heat. Reduce the heat, cover, and simmer 15-20 minutes, or until the largest potatoes are tender. Drain.

   For the dip, combine the sour cream, yogurt, chives, and thyme in a small bowl, mixing thoroughly with a fork. Season with salt and pepper.

   Place the small bowl in the middle of a warmed platter. Arrange the potatoes around it and spear each one with a toothpick for handling. Serve the potatoes hot.

Serves 4-6

TINY NEW POTATOES
WITH DILL PESTO

Pesto

1 cup loosely packed fresh dill
leaves

½ cup roughly chopped fresh
chives

½ cup grated sharp Cheddar
cheese

½ cup coarsely chopped
walnuts

¼ cup vegetable oil

2 tablespoons water

salt and freshly ground black
pepper, to taste

24-30 tiny new potatoes,
1 inch to 1½ inches in
diameter

My elderly neighbor is quite crippled with arthritis, yet each spring I see him making the painful effort to put in a couple of rows of Chieftain red potatoes. He says it's worth it just for tiny new potatoes in July.

This Dill Pesto is one of my favorite concoctions. It originated with another neighbor, David Hirsch, who wrote The Moosewood Restaurant Kitchen Garden. *Dill Pesto is delicious spread on toasted baguette slices and heated under a broiler and also makes a superb topping for baked potatoes.*

For the pesto, combine the dill, chives, cheese, and walnuts in a blender or food processer. Process until well mixed, then add the oil slowly in a thin stream to form a velvety smooth purée. Add the water, season with salt and pepper, and mix thoroughly.

For the potatoes, with the small end of a melon baller, scoop out a shallow depression in each potato. Steam the potatoes 15-20 minutes, or until tender.

Transfer the potatoes to a warmed serving plate and fill each depression with a generous dab of the pesto. Serve warm.

Serves 4-6

Note: The amount of salt you need will depend on the saltiness of the Cheddar cheese; you may need less than you think.

POTATO AND ROASTED RED PEPPER QUESADILLAS

2 medium potatoes
1 medium red bell pepper
1 large jalapeño chile
2 teaspoons vegetable oil
1 small onion, diced
2 cloves garlic, minced
1 tablespoon lime juice or red
   wine vinegar
1 tablespoon minced cilantro
½ cup cubed sharp Cheddar
   cheese
salt and freshly ground black
   pepper, to taste
four 6-inch flour tortillas

These quesadillas are such irresistible morsels that you may find yourself cooking up extra potatoes for dinner some night solely for the purpose of making them. Cut into small wedges, they are tempting appetizers. Cut into quarters, they make rewarding snacks and are a great comfort food. These can either be made ahead of time and reheated or assembled ahead of time and baked when needed.

Boil or steam the potatoes 35 minutes, or until tender. Allow them to cool, then peel and cut them into eighths.

Cut the bell and chile peppers in half vertically and remove the stems, seeds, and membranes. Slit each end so the peppers will lie as flat as possible, then place the halves skin side up on a broiler rack and position the rack close to the broiler. Broil the peppers until the skins are evenly charred and the flesh is tender, about 10 minutes. Remove, place the peppers in a paper bag or covered container, and seal. Set aside 15 minutes to steam and cool. (Doing this makes the peppers easier to peel.) With a paring knife, pull off and discard the charred skin, then dice the peppers.

Preheat the oven to 450°F.

Heat the oil in a large nonstick frying pan over medium-high heat. When hot, add the onions, garlic, and potatoes, and sauté until the onions and potatoes are lightly browned. Transfer to a bowl and mash briefly. Add the peppers, lime juice, cilantro, and cheese. Season with salt and pepper, and mix well.

Place 2 tortillas on an ungreased baking sheet. Place one-half of the potato mixture on each, and with a spatula, pat firmly to within ½ inch of the tortilla edge. Cover each tortilla with a second one and press firmly in place. Bake 5 minutes on each side. Cut each tortilla stack into 6 wedges and serve hot.

Yields 12 wedges; serves 4-6

Note: Instead of roasting a fresh red bell pepper, you could substitute one-half of a 7-ounce jar of roasted red peppers, drained.

Potato and Roasted Red Pepper Quesadillas (recipe this page)

ANTIPASTO PLATTER
WITH MANY HUED POTATOES

3 cups of ¾-inch cubes of
　　blue-, red-, yellow- and
　　white-fleshed potatoes

Vinaigrette
3 tablespoons extra-virgin
　　olive oil
3 tablespoons lemon juice
1 clove garlic, minced
1½ tablespoons minced fresh
　　basil, or 1 teaspoon dried

salt and freshly ground black
　　pepper, to taste

In Italian homes and restaurants, the antipasto platter is an institution. Antipasto, which translates to "before the meal," is an array of appetizers to whet the appetite and dull the pangs of hunger. It can range from just a couple of items to a grand spectacle. I like an antipasto platter because it offers the cook both convenience and a chance to shine with a particularly tasty dish or two. Many traditional antipasto offerings can be found canned or in the deli section of a supermarket.

Because blue- and red-fleshed potatoes have been on the scene a relatively short time, people who are unfamiliar with them are often taken aback. I always grow red-, blue- and yellow-fleshed potatoes and have devised this way of serving them. This platter is attractive, delicious, and always intrigues.

Place the potatoes in a steamer basket and steam about 15 minutes, or until all are tender.

For the vinaigrette, whisk together the oil, lemon juice, garlic, and basil in a small bowl or blender container.

Remove the potatoes from the heat and transfer them to a medium bowl. Gently mix in the vinaigrette. Season with salt and pepper. Let the flavors blend 1 hour before serving at room temperature.

Serves 4-6

Note: Other possibilities for an appetizing antipasto platter include sliced and rolled provolone cheese; pickled dill green beans; cubes of ripe melon wrapped in prosciutto; marinated artichoke hearts; marinated mushrooms; caponata (eggplant relish); an array of brined and oil-cured olives; sliced and rolled Genoa salami; roasted and marinated red peppers; pickled cocktail onions; pepperoncini; and cherry tomato halves spread with olivada (black olive spread). Most are commercially available, while recipes for others can be found in Italian cookbooks.

KERALIAN PASTRIES

Filling
4 medium potatoes
½ cup milk
1 tablespoon butter
1 tablespoon fresh dill, or
    1 teaspoon dried
salt and freshly ground black
    pepper, to taste

Dough
½ cup water
1 teaspoon salt
1 cup rye flour
¼ cup all-purpose flour

1 tablespoon butter
1 tablespoon water

*T*hese delightful, boat-shaped snacks originated in Keralia, a section of eastern Finland that was appropriated by the Soviet Union in 1940. They are popular treats in Finland, where the skill of a cook is tested by the thinness of the rolled rye-flour pastry. A Finnish friend tells me that she uses a pasta machine to achieve the required thinness. Keralian pastries are great out-of-hand food and are excellent for breakfast or lunch, with soup, as appetizers, or as a snack with juice, tea, or coffee.

For the filling, in a medium pot, cover the potatoes with water and bring to a boil over high heat. Reduce the heat, cover, and simmer 30-35 minutes, or until tender. Drain, let cool slightly, and peel.

In a medium bowl, mash the potatoes. Add the milk, butter, and dill, and season with salt and pepper. Cover and set aside.

For the dough, combine the water and salt in a medium bowl. Add the flours and mix to form a stiff dough. Turn the dough out onto a floured surface and knead until smooth and slightly elastic, 3-4 minutes. Form the dough into a 12-inch cylinder, then mark off and cut ¾-inch slices.

Press each slice into a circle between your palms. Place each circle on a floured pastry cloth or wax paper, press down, and flip it over so that the floured side is up. With a floured, sock-covered rolling pin, roll each piece into a paper-thin circle of 5 inches to 6 inches. Stack the circles on a plate and cover with a damp dish towel.

Preheat the oven to 475°F.

To assemble, place a heaping tablespoon of filling on each circle and spread into an oval shape, leaving 1 in. on the sides uncovered. Turn in the uncovered pastry edges over the filling and pleat them to nearly cover the filling, leaving a ¼-inch to ½-inch opening. Pat down the pleats to prevent them from burning. The height of the pastry should be no more than ½ inch.

Place the pastries on a large, ungreased baking sheet. Bake in the upper part of the oven 15-25 minutes, or until the bottoms of the pastries and the filling are browned.

In a small pot, melt the butter with the water over low heat. Brush the butter on the pastries while still hot from the oven. Serve warm.

Yields 13-14

CHINESE LATKES
WITH TANGY DIPPING SAUCE

2 medium potatoes
3 scallions, green and white
    parts, finely chopped
1 egg
1½ tablespoons cornstarch
1 teaspoon salt
2 tablespoons vegetable oil
Chinese Dipping Sauce,
    1 recipe

Chinese Dipping Sauce
1 teaspoon sesame seeds
1 small clove garlic, minced
1 scallion, green and white
    parts, finely chopped
4 tablespoons soy sauce
2 tablespoons white vinegar
2 teaspoons sesame oil
1 teaspoon sugar

*C*hinese latkes? Why not, in this era of fusion cooking? If Molly Goldberg had spent time in Peking, these are the potato pancakes that she would have cooked. The tangy Chinese Dipping Sauce replaces sour cream as a garnish and more than makes up for its absence. Make a lot of these latkes—they disappear quickly.

With a fine grater, grate the potatoes into a medium bowl. Add the scallions. In another bowl, beat the egg with the cornstarch and salt, then add to the potato mixture, stirring well.

In a large nonstick frying pan, heat 1 tablespoon of the oil over medium-high heat. When hot, drop a tablespoon of the potato mixture into the pan and flatten slightly with the back of the spoon. Continue making pancakes in this way until the pan is filled. Cook the pancakes 3-4 minutes on each side, or until lightly browned. Drain on paper towels. Add the remaining oil and cook the rest of the potato mixture in the same manner. Serve hot with the Chinese Dipping Sauce on the side.

Yields 12-15 small pancakes; serves 4

Chinese Dipping Sauce
In a toaster oven or heavy skillet, toast the sesame seeds over medium-high heat until slightly browned. Transfer the sesame seeds to a small bowl and add the remaining ingredients. Mix well. Serve at room temperature.

Yields ½ cup

Note: The recipe for the dipping sauce makes an ample amount, so even if you double the amount of pancakes, it should still be enough.

Chinese Latkes with Tangy Dipping Sauce (recipe this page)

NEW POTATO HALVES
WITH SHRIMP AND FETA TOPPING

10-12 small new potatoes

Topping
12-14 cooked medium shrimp
¼ cup crumbled feta cheese
1-2 teaspoons lemon juice
1 tablespoon sour cream
1 tablespoon drained capers, rinsed

Potatoes were first grown as food in the Andean highlands of what is now Peru. And from a wonderful Peruvian restaurant in Vancouver, British Columbia, comes the idea for this sumptuous dish, a creamy concoction of shrimp, feta cheese, and capers spread on sweet new potatoes.

In a large pot, cover the potatoes with water and bring to a boil over high heat. Lower the heat, cover, and simmer 15-20 minutes, or until tender. Remove the potatoes from the heat, drain, and let cool.

For the topping, place the shrimp, cheese, lemon juice, and sour cream in a food processer. Purée at high speed until smooth. Add the capers and process briefly, just long enough to blend them in.

Cut the potatoes in half and spread the cut half with the topping. Arrange on a platter and serve at room temperature.

Serves 6-8

ROASTED POTATO WEDGES
WITH RED PEPPER PURÉE

Potatoes
4 long, thin potatoes such as
    russets or White Rose
3 tablespoons olive oil
salt and freshly ground black
    pepper, to taste

Purée
1 tablespoon olive oil
1 medium onion, chopped
1 large clove garlic, minced
1 tablespoon balsamic vinegar
1 teaspoon chopped fresh
    basil
one 7-ounce jar roasted red
    peppers
tiny pinch of ground red
    pepper
salt and freshly ground black
    pepper, to taste

*T*his simple and delicious recipe has great visual appeal and is
easily multiplied for a crowd. These wedges are mighty tasty
when paired with kalamata or other flavorful olives.

For the potatoes, preheat the oven to 450°F. Peel the potatoes and cut lengthwise into quarters. Place them in a large, shallow bowl and toss with the oil and season with salt and pepper. Transfer the potatoes to a rimmed baking pan or sheet, arranging them in a single layer. Bake 30-35 minutes, or until browned and tender.

For the purée, in a medium frying pan, heat the oil over medium-high heat. When hot, add the onions and garlic and lower the heat. Cook over low heat 10 minutes, or until soft and golden. Transfer to a food processor or blender, and add the vinegar, basil, and the roasted red peppers and their liquid. Process until you have a smooth purée. Add the ground red pepper and season with salt and pepper, combining briefly. Serve at room temperature as a dip for the hot potato wedges.

Serves 4-6

Soups

Sweet-Sour Potato and Beet Soup
(recipe on page 74)

SWEET-SOUR POTATO AND BEET SOUP

2 medium-large potatoes
2 medium beets
6 cups water, or vegetable or
    chicken broth
1½ tablespoons vegetable oil
1 teaspoon caraway seeds
1 large onion, diced
1 large carrot, sliced
1 stalk celery, sliced
2 cups chopped cabbage
1 tablespoon fresh dill, or
    1 teaspoon dried
¼ cup tomato paste
¼ cup cider vinegar
3 tablespoons sugar
salt and freshly ground black
    pepper, to taste
low-fat plain yogurt, garnish

*T*his lovely crimson soup has a dual nature. In fall or winter, its heartiness comforts when served steaming hot with thin slices of pumpernickel and Jarlsburg cheese. In the summer, when thinned, puréed, and chilled, this soup offers tangy refreshment on a warm and muggy day. (Photo on page 72.)

Peel the potatoes, cut them in half lengthwise, and slice thinly. Peel the beets, cut them in half, and slice thinly. Place the potatoes and beets in a large saucepan, add the water or broth, and bring to a boil over high heat. Lower the heat and simmer gently.

While the potatoes and beets are cooking, heat the oil in a large frying pan over medium heat. When hot, add the caraway, onions, carrots, and celery, and sauté until the onions begin to brown. Stir in the cabbage and dill, and sauté 1 minute. Add this mixture to the potatoes and beets.

Stir in the tomato paste, vinegar, and sugar. Over high heat, bring to a boil. Lower the heat and simmer, partially covered, 45 minutes. Season with salt and pepper. Ladle into soup bowls and top with a dollop of yogurt.

Serves 4-6

Note: This soup can also be served cold. To do this, cool the soup slightly, then ladle it into a blender or food processor. Purée until smooth. Add some broth, water, half-and-half, or a combination to thin to the desired consistency. Garnish with a dollop of yogurt and minced fresh dill.

VICHYSSOISE

2 tablespoons butter
4 large leeks, well cleaned,
  white and pale green parts
  only
1 medium onion, chopped
4 large potatoes, peeled
1 stalk celery
3 cups chicken or vegetable
  broth
2 cups half-and-half
⅛ teaspoon freshly ground
  white pepper
salt, to taste
milk, for thinning
chopped chives, garnish

This velvety and refreshing chilled soup is almost easier to prepare than it is to pronounce (Vee-shee-swahz). It was developed in the early decades of this century by a French chef at the Ritz-Carlton Hotel in New York and named after Vichy, a spa near his childhood home.

In a soup pot, melt the butter over low heat. Slice the leeks thinly, then add them and the onions to the pot. Sauté, stirring occasionally, over low heat 10-15 minutes, or until softened and lightly browned.

Slice the potatoes and celery thinly, then add them and the broth to the pot. Stir to combine, and bring to a boil over high heat. Lower the heat and simmer, covered, 15-20 minutes, or until the potatoes are tender.

Remove the soup from the heat and cool slightly. In a blender, food processor, or food mill, purée the soup until smooth. Add the half-and-half and white pepper and season with salt. If necessary, thin with milk. Chill at least 4 hours in the refrigerator. Garnish with chives and serve in chilled bowls.

Serves 4-6

JOAN'S POTATO
AND CUCUMBER SOUP

1 large potato, or 2 medium,
   peeled and diced
2 cucumbers, peeled and diced
1 medium onion, sliced
3 cups chicken or vegetable
   broth
¾ cup low-fat plain yogurt
¾ cup low-fat milk
2 tablespoons lemon juice
1 tablespoon curry powder
salt and freshly ground black
   pepper, to taste
chopped scallions or cilantro,
   garnish

Potatoes and zesty seasonings give this soup a richness that belies its low-fat ingredients. Although this soup is heavenly on a warm summer day, I enjoy it just as much as a hot soup during the winter. It makes an especially nice first course.

In a soup pot, combine the potatoes, cucumbers, onions, and broth. Bring to a boil over high heat. Lower the heat, cover, and simmer 10-15 minutes, or until the potatoes are tender.

Remove the mixture from the heat, cool slightly, and ladle into a blender or food processor. Purée until completely smooth, then whisk in the yogurt, milk, lemon juice, and curry powder. Season with salt and pepper.

Allow the soup to cool slightly, then refrigerate 4-5 hours, or place it in the freezer at least 1 hour, until cold. Serve in chilled bowls topped with scallions or cilantro.

Serves 4-6

HUNGARIAN MUSHROOM
AND POTATO SOUP

2 tablespoons butter

1 medium onion, chopped

½ pound mushrooms, sliced

1 teaspoon paprika

2 tablespoons all-purpose flour

2 medium potatoes, peeled
  and diced

6 cups chicken or vegetable
  broth

2 teaspoons fresh dill, or
  ¾ teaspoon dried

⅓ cup chopped fresh parsley

¼ cup sherry or Madeira

2 bay leaves

½ cup low-fat sour cream, plus
  additional for garnish

salt and freshly ground black
  pepper, to taste

*In Hungary, as elsewhere in Europe, gathering mushrooms in the
fall is a hallowed tradition. Few people in this country seek out
flavorful wild mushrooms, but the increasing appearance in our
markets of fresh portobello and shiitake mushrooms presents a tasty
alternative to the common white ones that we are used to. Try this
soup with portobellos or fresh shiitakes if you can get them. If not, it's
still delicious with white mushrooms that are sautéed until golden
brown with onions, paprika, and dill.*

In a soup pot over medium-high heat, melt the butter, then sauté the onions, mushrooms, and paprika 5-10 minutes, or until the onions are translucent. Lower the heat, add the flour, and cook, stirring occasionally, 2-3 minutes. Add the potatoes, broth, dill, parsley, sherry or Madeira, and bay leaves. Over high heat, bring the mixture to a boil. Lower the heat, partially cover, and simmer gently 30-45 minutes.

Remove the soup from heat, and add the sour cream, whisking well to make sure that it is blended. Season with salt and pepper. Serve hot, garnishing with a dollop of additional sour cream, if desired.

Serves 4-6

INDIAN POTATO AND PEA SOUP

1 large potato, peeled and cut into chunks
1 medium onion, cut into chunks
6 cups vegetable or chicken broth
2 teaspoons grated fresh ginger
1½ teaspoons ground cumin
½ teaspoon ground coriander seeds
¼ cup chopped cilantro
pinch of ground red pepper
one 10-ounce package frozen peas
1-2 tablespoons lemon juice
1 teaspoon sugar
½ teaspoon *garam masala*
1 cup half-and-half
salt and freshly ground black pepper, to taste
thin slices of lemon, garnish

*S*oups are low-maintenance concoctions. One reason that I like to make them is that after the initial preparation, you can walk away and do something else while they simmer away. This smooth, fresh-green blend brings raves in winter as a hot soup or chilled as a piquant summer one.

In a soup pot, combine the potatoes, onions, broth, ginger, cumin, and coriander. Bring to a boil over high heat, then lower the heat and simmer, covered, 30 minutes. Add the cilantro, red pepper, and peas and simmer 2-3 minutes, or until the peas are tender. Remove from the heat and add the lemon juice, sugar, and *garam masala*.

Allow the soup to cool slightly, then purée it in a blender or food processor until smooth. Add the half-and-half, stirring to combine. Season with salt and pepper. Serve hot or cold, floating a slice of lemon on top as a garnish.

Serves 4-6

top: Potato-Chive Biscuits (recipe on page 157); bottom: Indian Potato and Pea Soup (recipe this page)

POTATO-GARLIC SOUP

1½ tablespoons vegetable oil
1 medium onion, chopped
9 large cloves garlic, chopped
2 stalks celery, sliced
6 medium baking or high-
    starch potatoes such as
    Yukon Gold, peeled and cut
    into eighths
6 cups chicken or vegetable
    broth
2 sprigs fresh thyme, or
    ½ teaspoon dried
1 cup half-and-half
salt and freshly ground black
    pepper, to taste
chopped fresh parsley, garnish

This is the soup that gives you the needed strength to get out there and start shoveling the 6 inches of wet snow that fell overnight. Don't be put off by the amount of garlic called for—chopping it by hand and simmering it for an hour or so mellows and rounds off its pungency.

In a soup pot, heat the oil over low heat. Sauté the onions, garlic, and celery until the onions are translucent and the garlic is golden. Add the potatoes, broth, and thyme and bring to a boil over high heat. Lower the heat and simmer, partially covered, 1 hour.

With a potato masher or slotted spoon, mash the potatoes. The soup should have a rustic rather than a refined texture. Add the half-and-half, and season with salt and pepper. Garnish with parsley and serve hot.

Serves 4-6

Note: Garlic is easy to chop by first mashing it on a cutting board. Do this by placing a clove under the flat blade of a large knife, such as a French chef's or Chinese cleaver, and smack the knife blade smartly with the heel of your fist. Peel, then chop the mashed clove.

POTATO AND POBLANO SOUP

2 tablespoons vegetable oil
3 cloves garlic, minced
1 medium onion, chopped
2-3 poblano chiles, roasted, peeled, and chopped
1 teaspoon ground cumin
6 cups chicken or vegetable broth
6 medium potatoes, peeled and coarsely chopped
1½-2 cups milk
1½-2 tablespoons lime juice
salt and freshly ground black pepper, to taste
chopped cilantro, garnish

*T*he fresh chile peppers that are turned into anchos by drying are called poblanos. Slightly hot, poblanos are the size of a medium bell pepper with a tapered heart shape. Their most distinguishing characteristic is their color, a glossy blackish green that is every bit as rich as their flavor. This soup is nicely complemented by a bean salad with southwestern seasonings and hot cornbread. It also makes a delicious chilled soup.

In a soup pot, heat the oil over medium heat. When hot, add the garlic, onions, chiles, and cumin. Sauté, stirring occasionally, until the onions begin to turn brown. Add the broth and potatoes and simmer, covered, 30 minutes.

Allow the soup to cool slightly, then transfer to a blender or food processor in several batches and purée until smooth. Return the soup to the pot and add milk to achieve the desired consistency. Add the lime juice, season with salt and pepper, and reheat. Garnish with cilantro and serve hot.

Serves 6-8

MEXICAN POTATO BROTH

4 cups chicken broth
1 ancho chile
1 medium-large boiling potato,
    peeled and cut into ¼-inch
    cubes
1 medium clove garlic, minced
1 cup corn kernels, fresh or
    frozen
1 tablespoon chopped cilantro
juice of ½ lime

Spring days in central New York state can be downright ugly—cold and rainy with cruel winds. One such raw day, I had a yen for a light but nourishing soup with warming Mexican overtones. Checking the larder, I came up with the ingredients for the following simple, quick, and satisfying soup. As I sipped it and tore off pieces of heated and buttered corn tortillas to eat, I mentally transported myself out of that ugly day and onto a sunny Oaxacan patio—travel by soup.

In a 3-quart pot, combine the broth, chile, potatoes, garlic, and corn. Over high heat, bring to a boil. Lower the heat and simmer, partially covered, 20-25 minutes. Remove the soup from the heat and remove the chile. Add the cilantro and lime juice. Serve hot.

Serves 3-4

Note: A well-flavored chicken broth is necessary for this soup. Homemade is the best, but Hain's makes a good canned version.

WINTER VEGETABLE SOUP

1 large potato, peeled and
    cubed (1½ cups)
2 large leeks, cleaned and cut
    into ½-inch slices (1½ cups)
1 large celeriac, peeled and
    cubed (3 cups)
8 cups water
¾ teaspoon dried tarragon
½-1 cup half-and-half
salt and freshly ground black
    pepper, to taste
chopped fresh parsley, garnish

What a lovely and soothing blend is this easily made soup. This is my version of a soup that David Cavagnaro, the horticultural photographer and gardener extraordinaire, described to me after a visit from a friend of his who is a chef. When invited for dinner, this friend likes to do the cooking, using David's garden produce as inspiration and ingredients. With potatoes, celeriac, and leeks from the root cellar, he created a fine soup that goes something like this.

In a soup pot, combine the potatoes, leeks, celeriac, water, and tarragon. Over high heat, bring to a boil. Lower the heat and simmer gently, covered, 1 hour. Remove the soup from the heat and cool slightly.

Purée the soup in batches in a blender or food processor until velvety smooth. Return the purée to the soup pot, then add the half-and-half until the desired consistency is reached. Season with salt and pepper. Serve hot, garnished with a sprinkling of parsley.

Serves 4-6

POTAGE OF POTATOES
AND TOMATOES

2 tablespoons olive oil
1 small onion, diced
2 cloves garlic, minced
2 teaspoons finely chopped
   fresh rosemary, or
   2 teaspoons grated fresh
   ginger
2 cups water, or vegetable or
   chicken broth
2 large, uncooked russet
   potatoes, peeled and diced
one 28-ounce can tomatoes,
   roughly puréed
salt and freshly ground black
   pepper, to taste
grated Parmesan cheese,
   garnish for potage with
   rosemary
minced cilantro, garnish for
   potage with ginger

*H*ere are two versions of a very simple and very delicious soup.
The procedure is the same for each soup, only the flavoring and
garnish differ. One version uses fresh rosemary and the other fresh
ginger to provide the main flavor note.

   *This soup is also fast to make, especially if you've got a couple of
leftover baked potatoes. Russets are a must because their mealiness
causes them to break up into a coarse purée when cooked in a liquid.
This recipe makes a hearty soup and can be made into a satisfying
meal accompanied by a green salad and some thick slices of a crusty
bread, lightly toasted.*

In a soup pot, heat the oil over medium heat. When hot, add the onions and garlic and sauté until golden. Add either the rosemary or ginger, and cook 2-3 minutes, or until the onions are lightly browned.

   Add the water or broth and the potatoes. Bring to a boil, lower the heat, and simmer, covered, 15 minutes, or until the potatoes are very tender. Crush the potatoes with a slotted spoon and add the tomatoes.

Simmer, covered, 10 minutes. Season with salt and pepper. Serve hot, adding the garnish to each soup bowl.

Serves 4-6

Note: If using previously baked potatoes, add the water or broth, potatoes, and tomatoes all at once. Simmer 10 minutes, then serve.

*top: Potato-Olive Bread
(recipe on page 160);
bottom: Potage of Potatoes and
Tomatoes (recipe this page)*

SCHAV

4 cups chicken or vegetable
    broth
2 medium boiling potatoes,
    peeled and cut into ¼-inch
    cubes
3 scallions, green and white
    parts, chopped, plus
    additional for garnish
3 cups stemmed and finely
    chopped sorrel
¼ cup fresh lemon juice
2 tablespoons brown sugar
1 tablespoon fresh dill, or
    1 teaspoon dried, plus
    additional fresh for garnish
2 eggs
1 cup cold water
salt and freshly ground black
    pepper, to taste
1 cup low-fat sour cream
finely chopped cucumbers or
    hard-boiled eggs, garnish

This soup is the reason that I grow sorrel, a rough-looking assemblage of lance-shaped leaves that are at their best in spring and fall. Sorrel has a marvelous tartness that calls out for the soothing comfort of potatoes.

Traditionally this soup is served chilled, but I like it hot just as well. My favorite things to have with schav are thin slices of pumpernickel bread spread with sweet butter and sparkling, crisp radishes.

In a soup pot, bring the broth, potatoes, and scallions to a boil over high heat. Lower the heat and simmer 5 minutes. Add the sorrel, lemon juice, brown sugar, and dill, and simmer, partially covered, 10 minutes, or until the potatoes are tender.

In a large bowl, beat the eggs with the water. Slowly add the hot soup, whisking constantly so the soup doesn't curdle. Season with salt and pepper, then whisk in the sour cream.

Chill thoroughly at least 4 hours, then ladle into bowls. Before serving, sprinkle one or two garnishes over the top of each soup bowl.

Serves 6

Note: To stem sorrel, grip the stem end with one hand, and with the other pull the leaf away from the rib. If the leaves are very large, fold them in half, lay on a cutting board, and separate the leaf from the rib with a sharp knife.

CHICKEN VEGETABLE SOUP
WITH POTATO DUMPLINGS

Soup

6 cups chicken broth

1-2 scallions, green and white
parts, finely chopped

1 teaspoon fresh thyme, or
¼ teaspoon dried

1 tablespoon chopped fresh
parsley

1 teaspoon fresh dill, or
½ teaspoon dried

½ cup thinly sliced carrots

½ cup thinly sliced celery

1 medium boiling potato, cut
into ½-inch cubes

1 cup sliced mushrooms

salt and freshly ground black
pepper, to taste

Dumplings

1 cup mashed potatoes
(1 large or 1½ medium
potatoes)

¼ cup flour

3 tablespoons finely chopped
scallions, green and white
parts

3 tablespoons chopped fresh
parsley

1 egg, beaten

¼ teaspoon nutmeg

½ teaspoon salt

⅛-¼ teaspoon freshly ground
black pepper

*T*ake a classic chicken soup with vegetables, add meltingly tender
potato dumplings, and you've got solace for wintertime blues,
heartbreak, or a phone that's been too silent too long. The secret to
delicious potato dumplings is to keep the cooking liquid at a simmer. If
it boils, there is the risk of dumpling disintegration—not a pretty sight.

For the soup, in a soup pot, combine the broth, scallions, thyme, parsley, and dill. Bring to a boil over high heat. Add the carrots, celery, and potatoes, then lower the heat and simmer 15 minutes. Add the mushrooms and simmer 10 minutes.

For the dumplings, heat 3 quarts of salted water to simmering in a large pot.

In a medium bowl, combine the potatoes, flour, scallions, parsley, egg, nutmeg, salt, and pepper. Scooping with a tablespoon, form the dough into 12 balls. Lower the dumplings into the water and simmer gently, covered, 10 minutes.

Remove the dumplings with a slotted spoon and divide them among shallow soup bowls. Ladle the soup over the dumplings and serve hot.

Serves 4-6

Salads

Russian Salad (recipe on page 90)

RUSSIAN SALAD

2 cups cooked, peeled, and
    diced boiling potatoes,
    slightly cooled
2 cups cooked, peeled, and
    diced beets, slightly cooled
1 cup peeled, seeded, and
    diced cucumber (1 medium)
½ cup minced onions
1 tart apple, peeled and diced
1 cup minced dill pickles
Sharp and Creamy Dressing,
    1 recipe
salt and freshly ground black
    pepper, to taste

Sharp and Creamy Dressing
½ cup low-fat plain yogurt
½ cup low-fat mayonnaise
2 tablespoons cider vinegar
1-2 tablespoons finely
    chopped fresh dill
1 teaspoon Dijon mustard

*T*here are many versions of Russian Salad, but the common
denominator in all seems to be potatoes—potatoes combined with
other cooked and fresh vegetables in a tangy and creamy dressing.
This rosy-hued Russian Salad makes a nice Sunday night supper with
some crusty pumpernickel, Swiss cheese, and a bowl of applesauce.
(Photo on page 88.)

In a large bowl, mix the potatoes,
beets, cucumbers, onions, apples,
and pickles. Add the dressing,
stirring to combine. Season with salt
and pepper. Serve immediately.

Serves 6

*Note: If making this salad ahead of
time, keep the beets separate from the
other vegetables. Add them just before
serving, when mixing in the dressing.*

Sharp and Creamy Dressing
In a small bowl, whisk together
or beat the yogurt, mayonnaise,
vinegar, dill, and mustard.

BLUE POTATO
AND ARTICHOKE SALAD

6 medium blue-fleshed or
   other boiling potatoes
Oregano Vinaigrette, 1 recipe
one 14-ounce can artichoke
   bottoms or hearts
18 kalamata olives, pitted and
   sliced
salt and freshly ground black
   pepper, to taste

Oregano Vinaigrette
¼ cup wine vinegar
¼ cup olive oil
¾ teaspoon Dijon mustard
3 tablespoons chopped fresh
   oregano, or 1 teaspoon
   dried

*T*his is a delectable lavender-tinted potato salad with a Mediterranean accent. As in any salad, the quality of ingredients makes a noticeable difference. A good green and fruity olive oil will impart the finest flavor. I also like to use fresh oregano for the subtlety of its taste; it doesn't overpower the artichokes.

In a large pot, cover the potatoes with water and bring to a boil over high heat. Lower the heat, cover, and simmer 30 minutes, or until tender. Remove the potatoes from heat and drain. Peel the potatoes and cut them into ½-inch to ¾-inch chunks. Place them in a medium-large bowl.

Pour the vinaigrette over the potatoes, and stir to combine. Drain the artichokes, quarter them, then stir them and the olives into the potato mixture. Season with salt and pepper. Serve at room temperature.

Serves 4-6

Oregano Vinaigrette

In a small bowl, whisk together the vinegar, oil, mustard, and oregano.

ROASTED POTATO SALAD

3 small cloves garlic, minced

5 tablespoons olive oil

3 medium boiling or all-purpose potatoes, peeled and cut into ½-inch cubes

1 small eggplant, peeled and cut into ½-inch cubes

1 large red bell pepper, cut into ½-inch strips

1 medium purple onion, halved and cut into ½-inch-thick slices

salt and freshly ground black pepper, to taste

1 heaping tablespoon minced fresh basil or oregano

1-2 tablespoons balsamic vinegar

A wonderful transformation occurs when fleshy vegetables are roasted. They develop a rich, browned flavor, and their natural sweetness comes to the fore. In this recipe, potatoes, eggplant, red bell pepper, and purple onion are tossed with garlic and olive oil before roasting and finished off with balsamic vinegar and fresh herbs before serving. I divide the oil and add it in two steps because eggplants are like sponges and will sop up all the oil you give them.

Preheat the oven to 375°F. Lightly oil 2 large, rimmed baking sheets.

In a large bowl, mix 2 of the garlic cloves with 3 tablespoons of the oil. Add the potatoes and eggplant, and stir to thoroughly coat. Transfer to a baking sheet and arrange in a single layer.

In the same bowl, mix the remaining oil with the remaining garlic. Add the peppers and onions, and stir to thoroughly coat. Transfer to the second baking sheet in a single layer. Season all the vegetables with salt and pepper, then roast 35-40 minutes, or until tender.

With a spatula, transfer the vegetables to a large bowl. Toss with the basil or oregano and vinegar. Serve warm or at room temperature.

Serves 4

SPRINGTIME POTATO
AND ASPARAGUS SALAD

4 cups halved or quartered
   tiny new red potatoes, or
   6 peeled medium boiling
   potatoes, cut into ½-inch
   cubes
1 bunch asparagus, cut into
   1-inch pieces (3 cups)
Lemon-Chive Vinaigrette,
   1 recipe
salt and freshly ground black
   pepper, to taste

Lemon-Chive Vinaigrette
¼ cup freshly squeezed lemon
   juice
¼ cup olive oil
1 clove garlic, minced
3 tablespoons minced chives

I find that this recipe benefits from steaming the potatoes over an aromatic liquid (see page 52). The flavoring ingredients that I like to add to the steaming liquid are a sprig of rosemary, a couple of crushed garlic cloves, freshly ground black pepper, and half a lemon, quartered and squeezed into the liquid.

Steam the potatoes 20 minutes, or until tender, then transfer them to a large bowl. Steam the asparagus 2-3 minutes, or until barely tender. Add to the potatoes. Pour the vinaigrette over the potatoes and asparagus and mix well. Season with salt and pepper. Serve at room temperature.

Serves 6

Lemon-Chive Vinaigrette
In a small bowl, whisk together the lemon juice, oil, garlic, and chives.

POTATO AND ROASTED
RED PEPPER SALAD

8 medium boiling potatoes
2 large red bell peppers
12 kalamata olives, pitted and
    quartered
¼ cup chopped fresh basil
Lemon-Garlic Vinaigrette,
    1 recipe
salt and freshly ground black
    pepper, to taste

Lemon-Garlic Vinaigrette
⅓ cup extra-virgin olive oil
⅓ cup lemon juice
1 clove garlic, minced

*W*ith the red of the roasted peppers, purple-black of the olives, and vivid green of the basil, this makes an eye-catching potato salad and is always a hit.

In a large pot, cover the potatoes with water and bring to a boil. Lower the heat, cover, and simmer 30-40 minutes, or until tender. Drain in a colander.

Cut the peppers in half vertically and remove the stems, seeds, and membranes. Cut a 1-inch slit in the blossom end of each pepper half and press as flat as possible. Place the peppers on a broiler rack, then broil until the skins are evenly charred and the flesh is tender, about 10 minutes. Remove the peppers and place them in a paper bag or covered container and seal. Set aside 15 minutes to steam and cool. (This makes the peppers easier to peel.) With a paring knife,

peel off and discard the skin, then chop the peppers into ¾-inch squares.

Peel the potatoes and cut them into ½-inch to ¾-inch cubes. In a large bowl, mix the potatoes, peppers, olives, and basil. Add the vinaigrette, stirring to combine. Season with salt and pepper. Let the salad sit at room temperature 2-3 hours to allow the flavors to marry. Serve at room temperature.

Serves 6-8

Lemon-Garlic Vinaigrette

In a small bowl, whisk together the oil, lemon juice, and garlic.

*Potato and Roasted Red Pepper
Salad (recipe this page)*

WARM GERMAN POTATO SALAD
WITH SAUSAGE

1 tablespoon butter
3 tablespoons vegetable oil
4 medium red onions, thinly
    sliced (4 cups)
2 teaspoons fresh thyme, or
    ¾ teaspoon dried
1 teaspoon caraway seeds
6 medium fingerling potatoes
½ pound low-fat kielbasa
2 tablespoons cider vinegar
2 tablespoons brown sugar
½ teaspoon Dijon mustard
salt and freshly ground black
    pepper, to taste
chopped fresh dill, garnish

*T*his mouth-watering sweet-sour dish is a perfect vehicle for finger-ling potatoes, which remain firm when cooked. When fingerlings are sliced, their shape makes a nice match for the kielbasa. For an entrée, serve this salad with a fresh green salad and thinly sliced pumpernickel and Muenster cheese.

In a large frying pan, heat the butter and 1 tablespoon of the oil over medium-high heat. Add the onions, thyme, and caraway. Sauté 2-3 minutes, or until the onions begin to soften. Lower the heat, cover, and cook, stirring occasionally, 20-30 minutes, or until the onions are tender but not browned.

While the onions are cooking, place the potatoes in a large pot, cover with water, and bring to a boil over high heat. Lower the heat and simmer, covered, 15 minutes. Pierce the kielbasa several times with a fork, add to the potatoes, and simmer 10 minutes, turning several times. Drain, cool slightly, then slice the potatoes and kielbasa into ½-inch pieces. Place in a large bowl.

In a small bowl, whisk together the remaining oil, vinegar, brown sugar, and mustard. Season with salt and pepper. Drizzle this mixture over the potatoes and kielbasa and mix well. Arrange the onions on a serving platter and top with the potato mixture. Sprinkle with dill and serve warm.

Serves 4

TINY NEW POTATOES WITH PARSLEY AND MUSTARD DRESSING

24 tiny new potatoes, 1 inch to
    1½ inches in diameter
¼ cup chopped fresh parsley
Mustard Dressing, 1 recipe
salt and freshly ground black
    pepper, to taste

Mustard Dressing
2 tablespoons Dijon mustard
2 tablespoons cider vinegar
1 clove garlic, minced
¼ cup extra-virgin olive oil

This felicitous combination of tender new potatoes and parsley with a tangy mustard dressing is good anytime, anyplace. True potato lovers have been seen dipping into this with breakfast, but the more orthodox can successfully serve this dish with barbecued chicken or polenta with savory, cooked greens. Like all potato salads, this is great picnic food. As well as this dish's fabulous flavor, another asset is its speed and ease of preparation. When I have to make a potato salad in a hurry, this is the one I make.

In a large pot, cover the potatoes with water and bring to a boil over high heat. Lower the heat and simmer, covered, 15-20 minutes, or until tender. Remove from the heat and drain. Cut the potatoes in half, then place in a medium serving bowl.

Add the parsley and dressing to the potatoes. Season with salt and pepper and stir gently to combine. Serve at room temperature.

Serves 4

Mustard Dressing

In a small bowl, whisk together the mustard, vinegar, and garlic. Gradually whisk in the oil until the dressing is completely blended.

MEXICAN FIESTA POTATO SALAD

4 medium boiling potatoes
1 cup fresh or frozen corn
    kernels
Lime Juice Vinaigrette, 1 recipe
1-2 jalapeño chiles, minced
½ medium red bell pepper,
    diced
½ medium green bell pepper,
    diced
½ cup finely chopped red
    onions
2 tablespoons chopped
    cilantro
salt and freshly ground black
    pepper, to taste

Lime Juice Vinaigrette
¼ cup lime juice
¼ cup olive oil
½ teaspoon ground coriander
    seeds
½ teaspoon ground cumin

Years ago as a college student, I had a basic art textbook titled Color, Form and Texture. When I put this colorful salad together, those basic elements came to mind. At first bite a necessary element in culinary art came to mind—marvelous taste.

In a large pot, cover the potatoes with water and bring to a boil over high heat. Lower the heat, cover, and simmer 25-30 minutes, or until tender. Remove from the heat, drain, and cool slightly. Peel and cut the potatoes into ½-inch to ¾-inch cubes. Cook the corn 2-3 minutes, drain, and refresh under cold running water.

In a large bowl, combine the potatoes and corn, then mix in the vinaigrette. Add the chiles, peppers, onions, and cilantro. Season with salt and pepper and mix well. Serve at room temperature or slightly chilled.

Serves 4-6

Lime Juice Vinaigrette
In a small bowl, whisk together the lime juice, oil, coriander, and cumin.

POTATO SALAD
WITH MINT AND CAPERS

6 medium boiling potatoes
¼ cup extra-virgin olive oil
¼ cup red wine vinegar
1 clove garlic, minced
½ teaspoon dried oregano
⅓ cup chopped fresh mint
  leaves
2 tablespoons drained capers,
  rinsed
salt and freshly ground black
  pepper, to taste
1 large tomato, garnish

*T*his unusual combination of fresh aromatic mint, capers with
their salty zing, and the comfortable neutrality of potatoes is
something that I find irresistible. This salad is marvelous with
anything from the grill.

In a large pot, cover the potatoes with water and bring to a boil over high heat. Lower the heat, cover, and simmer 30-35 minutes, or until tender. Drain and cool slightly. Peel and cut the potatoes into ¾-inch cubes and place them in a medium bowl.

While the potatoes are cooking, place the oil, vinegar, garlic, oregano, and mint in a blender or food processor. Process at high speed until the mint is finely chopped.

Pour the dressing over the potatoes and toss to thoroughly combine. Stir in the capers and season with salt and pepper. Cut the tomato into wedges for garnish. Serve at room temperature.

Serves 4

FRENCH POTATO SALAD

8 medium boiling potatoes
¾ cup chopped mixed fresh
   herbs (chives, dill, arugula,
   basil, marjoram, oregano,
   chervil, summer savory,
   rosemary, thyme, parsley)
¼-⅓ cup extra-virgin olive oil
¼-⅓ cup white wine vinegar
salt and freshly ground black
   pepper, to taste

This is the potato salad that signifies summer to me. It is the simplest and freshest of potato salads, and like most simple dishes, its success depends on the quality of its ingredients. In this case, a good fruity olive oil, white wine vinegar, and savory, chopped fresh herbs are essential.

Although the combination of herbs depends upon what is available, here are some favorites. Arugula, chives, basil, and rosemary give a definite and delicious Mediterranean accent. Chives, dill, Italian parsley, and tarragon are also lovely. Remember to balance strongly flavored herbs such as rosemary, tarragon, and sage with generous amounts of milder herbs like parsley and chives.

In a large pot, cover the potatoes with water and bring to a boil over high heat. Lower the heat, cover, and simmer 30-35 minutes, or until tender. Drain and cool slightly. Peel and slice the potatoes, then place them in a large, shallow bowl.

Sprinkle the herbs over the potatoes. In a small bowl, whisk together the oil and vinegar, then pour over the potatoes and herbs.

Toss gently to combine, and season with salt and pepper. Let sit 1 hour at room temperature before serving to allow the flavors to develop.

Serves 4-6

Note: For the best flavor in a potato salad, add the herbs and the oil and vinegar while the potatoes are still warm.

WATERCRESS AND HERB SALAD
WITH POTATO CROUTONS

1 clove garlic
6 cups loosely packed,
   washed, trimmed, and dried
   watercress or fresh spinach
4 cups loosely packed,
   washed, and dried mixed
   herb sprigs and leaves (dill,
   Italian parsley, fennel,
   chervil, tarragon, spearmint,
   oregano, basil, arugula,
   cilantro)
2 medium russet potatoes,
   peeled and cut into ½-inch
   cubes
vegetable oil for frying
salt and freshly ground black
   pepper, to taste
Lemon Vinaigrette, 1 recipe

Lemon Vinaigrette
¼ cup extra-virgin olive oil
2 tablespoons white wine
   vinegar
1 tablespoon lemon juice
2 tablespoons minced shallots
   or mild onions
salt and freshly ground black
   pepper, to taste

*S*erving a bowlful of fresh salad greens with bits of flavorful, sautéed or toasted bread croutons is a time-honored method of adding interest to a salad. I think this recipe is even better. A layer of crisp and succulent fried potato cubes is nestled on a tasty combination of watercress and fresh herbs tossed with a lemony vinaigrette. The contrast in tastes and textures is marvelous. This recipe is adapted from one in Maggie Waldron's fine book, Potatoes, A Country Garden Cookbook.

Cut the garlic in half and rub the inside of a large salad bowl with it. Discard the garlic. With clean hands, toss the watercress and herbs in the bowl. Cover and refrigerate.

Heat ¼ inch to ½ inch oil in an 8-inch frying pan over medium-high heat. The oil should be hot but not smoking and should immediately bubble around a test cube of potato. Fry the potatoes in two batches, turning and removing them with a slotted spoon to drain on paper towels. Season with salt and pepper.

To serve, toss the watercress and herbs with the vinaigrette. Divide among four plates and top with the potatoes.

Serves 4

Note: The greens and potatoes can be prepared ahead of time. To serve, reheat the potatoes in a toaster oven. Toss the greens with the vinaigrette and top with the potatoes.

Lemon Vinaigrette
In a small bowl, whisk together the oil, vinegar, lemon juice, and shallots. Season with salt and pepper.

Side Dishes

Colcannon (recipe on page 104)

COLCANNON

5 medium potatoes
4 cups packed, rinsed kale
    leaves with stems removed
2 tablespoons vegetable oil
1 cup chopped leeks
2 large onions
2 tablespoons butter
½-¾ cup warm milk
salt and freshly ground black
    pepper, to taste

*W*ith the cool-season vegetables of potatoes, kale, and leeks as its main ingredients, this dish from the British Isles is a reward waiting at the end of the growing season. The topping of browned onions turns this reward into a north country ambrosia. Any leftovers make great potato patties sautéed on each side in a little butter.

I like to use a variety of kale called Russian Red for this recipe. It has a tender mildness and a pleasing flavor. Its leaves are smoother than the more common Scotch kale and have a reddish tinge on the edges and veins. (Photo on page 102.)

Boil or steam the potatoes 30-45 minutes, or until completely tender. Allow the potatoes to cool, then peel them.

While the potatoes are cooking, steam the kale 5 minutes. Drain, squeeze out the excess water, and chop the kale finely.

In a large frying pan, heat the oil over medium heat. When hot, add the leeks and sauté 5 minutes, or until tender. Lower the heat, add the kale, and sauté 5-10 minutes, stirring occasionally.

Peel and cut the onions in half vertically. With the flat side on a chopping block, cut each half vertically into semicircular slices. In a medium frying pan, melt the butter over medium-low heat. When hot, add the onions and cook slowly 15-20 minutes, or until the onions are limp and browned.

To assemble, mash the potatoes with a potato ricer or masher, adding enough milk to make a creamy yet firm mixture. Beat in the kale and leek mixture, and season with salt and pepper.

To serve, reheat if necessary. Turn into a heated serving bowl, make a large, shallow depression in the middle, and fill with the onions.

Serves 4-6

TUSCAN POTATO PATTIES

4 medium boiling potatoes
⅓ cup dry breadcrumbs
½ cup chopped roasted red
    peppers
¼ cup minced fresh basil
½ cup pitted, chopped
    kalamata or other flavorful
    olives
½ cup of ¼-inch cubes of aged
    provolone cheese
salt and freshly ground black
    pepper, to taste
¼-⅓ cup cornmeal
1½ tablespoons olive oil

In this dish, a crisp cornmeal crust encloses a chunky potato interior redolent with fresh basil, roasted red pepper, flavorful olives, and provolone cheese. Although these patties are a pleasing companion to many main dishes, they also make a fine entrée, especially in company with a simple fresh tomato sauce.

This recipe calls for roasted fresh red peppers because of their fine taste. However, since roasting them is a time-consuming process, canned roasted red peppers can be substituted.

In a medium pot, cover the potatoes with water and bring to a boil over high heat. Lower the heat, cover, and simmer 30-35 minutes, or until tender. Remove from the heat, drain, and cool slightly. Peel the potatoes, cut them into chunks, and place them in a large bowl.

With a potato masher, mash the potatoes until they are generally smooth but retain enough small chunks to add texture. Add the breadcrumbs, peppers, basil, olives, and cheese. Season with salt and pepper. Mix thoroughly and form into 6 patties.

Pour the cornmeal into a shallow bowl. Dredge each patty in the cornmeal, then place on a plate.

In a large nonstick frying pan, heat the oil over medium heat. When hot, add the patties and cook 4-5 minutes on each side, or until browned. Serve hot.

Yields six 3-inch patties

Note: You can get a head start on this dish by cooking the potatoes ahead of time, then adding the remaining ingredients just before cooking.

VARIATIONS ON A
MASHED POTATO THEME

Spanish Mashed

4 large potatoes, preferably
    russets
1 tablespoon olive oil
2 large cloves garlic, minced
pinch of saffron
one 14-ounce can tomatoes,
    drained
salt and freshly ground black
    pepper, to taste

Garlic Mashed

4 large potatoes, preferably
    russets
1 medium head garlic
2 tablespoons butter
½ cup heavy cream
salt and freshly ground black
    pepper, to taste
additional butter and hot milk,
    optional

Irish Mashed

1 large celeriac, or 1 medium
    parsnip
4 medium potatoes, preferably
    russets, peeled and cut into
    1-inch cubes
⅓ cup milk
2 tablespoons butter
salt and freshly ground black
    pepper, to taste

For many people, a mound of mashed potatoes heads the list of comfort foods. If you're looking for a tasty side dish that goes beyond Classic Mashed (see page 53), try one of these.

Spanish Mashed

These sunset-colored mashed potatoes have a slight piquancy and are marvelous with a light chicken, fish, or cheese entrée. For ease of handling, I like to grind saffron with a small amount of sugar using a mortar and pestle.

In a medium pot, cover the potatoes with water and bring to a boil. Lower the heat and simmer 30-45 minutes, or until tender. Drain, peel, and cut the potatoes into chunks, then place in a large, warmed bowl.

While the potatoes are cooking, heat the oil in a heavy-bottomed, medium saucepan over low heat. Sauté the garlic until it begins to turn golden, then stir in the saffron and tomatoes. Heat just to the boiling point, then add to the potatoes.

With an electric mixer, combine the potatoes with the tomato mixture, processing until smooth. Season with salt and pepper. Serve hot.

Serves 4-6

Garlic Mashed

This fragrant recipe originated with Julia Child and, as many of her dishes are, is rich and delicious. The taste of the garlic is softened by gently cooking it in butter and cream.

In a medium pot, cover the potatoes with water and bring to a boil. Lower the heat and simmer 30-45 minutes, or until tender. Drain, peel, and cut the potatoes into chunks.

While the potatoes are cooking, separate the cloves from the head of garlic and peel. In a small saucepan, melt the butter over the lowest possible heat. Add the garlic and cook, covered, 5-7 minutes, or until creamy yellow. Turn the cloves so that they cook evenly, and do not allow them to brown. Add the cream, cover, and simmer gently over the lowest heat 10 minutes, or until the garlic is tender.

Purée the garlic mixture in a food processor or blender.

In a large bowl, rice or mash the potatoes. Add the garlic purée and continue to mash. Season with salt and pepper. Add more butter and hot milk, if desired.

Serves 4-6

Irish Mashed

One potato-loving guest declared this dish "awesome" and there was a general murmur of agreement. It is wonderful with baked ham, a vegetable ragout, or roast chicken. Do not be put off by the unattractive dun color and gnarliness of celeriac. Inside there is fine-textured, white flesh tasting of celery and walnuts.

Prepare the celeriac by slicing off the stem end with a sharp paring knife. Pare the thick skin and rootlets as you would an orange rind, slicing from top to bottom. Cut into 1-inch chunks. If you are using parsnip, prepare it by peeling with a vegetable peeler and cutting it into ¾-inch-thick slices.

Place the potatoes and celeriac or parsnip in a large pot and cover with water. Over high heat, bring to a boil. Lower the heat, cover, and simmer 20 minutes, or until tender.

In a small saucepan, combine the milk and butter and heat over medium-low heat until the butter is melted and the milk is hot.

Drain the vegetables. With a ricer or potato masher, press or mash the vegetables into a large heated bowl. Add the milk and butter and stir to combine. Season with salt and pepper and serve hot.

Serves 4-6

POTATO AND LEEK GRATIN

1 clove garlic
1 teaspoon olive oil
3 leeks
6 medium boiling or
    all-purpose potatoes
1 teaspoon fresh thyme, or
    ¼ teaspoon dried
salt and freshly ground black
    pepper, to taste
1½ cups half-and-half, or
    vegetable or chicken broth
1 cup grated Cheddar, Swiss,
    or Parmesan cheese

*P*otatoes are like blank canvases. Add seasonings, mess around *with their texture and preparation method, and the possibilities are endless. Perfect examples of this versatility are potato gratins. At its most basic, a gratin is a dish baked slowly in a wide, shallow baking pan, usually ceramic. Its ingredients are often thinly sliced vegetables, and most often, those vegetables are potatoes. Since potatoes lend themselves so well to combinations, try layering them in a gratin with other ingredients. Some of my favorites are sliced parsnip or celeriac, browned onion slices, chopped sorrel, chard, or kale, and a sprinkle of sliced kalamata olives.*

Slice the garlic in half and rub the cut edges around the sides and bottom of a 10-inch to 12-inch gratin dish (one that holds 5-6 cups). Coat the dish with the oil.

Preheat the oven to 375°F.

Remove the tough outer leaves from the leeks and remove the root end. Rinse well, then slice the tender white and pale green sections ⅛ inch thick.

Peel the potatoes and slice them ⅛ inch thick.

In the gratin pan, layer overlapping slices of the potato. Season with salt and pepper, then sprinkle with one-half of the thyme and one-half of the leeks. Repeat these layers once, then cover with a potato layer and season with salt and pepper.

Pour the half-and-half or broth until it reaches just below the top layer of potatoes. Place the gratin dish on a baking sheet and bake 30 minutes. Sprinkle with the cheese and bake another 15-30 minutes, or until the potatoes are tender and nicely browned. Serve hot.

Serves 6

*Potato and Leek Gratin
(recipe this page)*

GRILLED ROSEMARY AND GARLIC POTATOES

¼ cup olive oil
1 tablespoon minced fresh
    rosemary, or 1 teaspoon
    dried
3 cloves garlic, minced
2 tablespoons balsamic vinegar
1 teaspoon salt
½ teaspoon freshly ground
    black pepper
4 large russet potatoes

There is probably no cooking method as thoroughly American as grilling outdoors. In many backyards across the country, the family altar of the carefully constructed brick barbecue of the '50s can still be seen. These have become relics since the advent of the easier-to-use covered kettle grill and the popular gas grill. Since the potatoes used in this dish cook away from the direct heat of the hot coals, they are a perfect accompaniment to a grilled meat or fish entrée.

Light a pile of charcoal on one side of a grill or fire up one burner on a gas grill.

Combine the oil, rosemary, garlic, vinegar, salt, and pepper in a blender or by whisking by hand in a small bowl. Set aside.

Peel the potatoes and quarter them lengthwise. Pour the oil mixture into a shallow dish, then roll the potatoes in it until they are thoroughly coated.

When the charcoal is covered with a light gray ash, put the potatoes on the grill away from the heat. Cover the grill and cook the potatoes until tender, turning them every 10 minutes to cook evenly. If you have extra oil mixture, brush it on the potatoes as they grill. Depending on their size, the potatoes will take 20-40 minutes to cook. When a fork easily pushes through the thickest part of the potatoes, they are ready. Remove them from the grill and serve hot.

Serves 4-6

POTATOES WITH ARUGULA AND HERBS

6 medium boiling potatoes

4 tablespoons extra-virgin olive oil

salt and freshly ground black pepper, to taste

1 small bunch arugula, chopped (1 cup loosely packed)

1½ tablespoons chopped fresh basil

3 tablespoons chopped flat-leaf parsley

kalamata or oil-cured black olives, garnish

lemon wedges, garnish

*A*rugula may be most familiar in its salad role, where its distinct flavor adds pizzazz to any collection of greens. It also makes a marvelous seasoning herb, as in this fresh-tasting dish of potato cubes tossed in a fruity olive oil that is verdant with bits of chopped greens—basil, Italian parsley, and the arugula. Serve this summery side dish, which is adapted from one in Verduras by Viana La Place, with grilled meat or fish or with a chilled soup and a garden salad.

In a large pot, cover the potatoes with water and bring to a boil. Lower the heat and simmer, covered, 30-35 minutes, or until tender. Drain, cool slightly, and peel. Cut the potatoes into ¾-inch cubes and place in a medium serving bowl.

Add the oil, and season with salt and pepper, stirring gently to combine. Add the arugula, basil, and parsley, and mix in gently. Serve warm or at room temperature, garnished with olives and lemon wedges, if desired.

Serves 4

BAKED ROSEMARY, ONION, AND POTATO CAKE

2 tablespoons olive oil
3-4 medium onions, sliced thin
4 medium potatoes
1-1½ tablespoons chopped
    fresh rosemary
salt and freshly ground black
    pepper, to taste
1 cup half-and-half

Although fresh rosemary is used in this dish, dill, basil, tarragon, or thyme would also be delicious. This is a rich and savory dish, and I often enjoy it as an entrée with fresh green beans or peas and a marinated vegetable salad.

In a large frying pan, heat the oil over medium-high heat. When hot, add the onions. Lower the heat, and cook slowly 15-20 minutes, or until the onions are soft and golden.

Preheat the oven to 375°F.

Oil a 9-inch pie pan or shallow casserole. Peel the potatoes and slice them very thin. Divide the potatoes, onions, and rosemary into thirds. Place a layer of one-third of the potatoes in the pie pan, then add a layer of one-third of the onions, and top with one-third of the rosemary. Season with salt and pepper. Continue in this manner, ending with rosemary, salt, and pepper. Pour in the half-and-half, cover with aluminum foil or a lid, place on a baking sheet, and bake 45 minutes. Uncover and bake another 20 minutes, or until the potatoes are tender and browned. Serve hot.

Serves 4-6

ROASTY POTATOES WITH SAGE

8-10 small boiling potatoes
2 tablespoons extra-virgin
  olive oil
30-40 fresh sage leaves
2 teaspoons salt

A crisp, roasted sage leaf or two embosses the cut surface of each roasted potato chunk and gives this dish great eye appeal. The roasting mellows the assertive taste of sage to just a suggestion. Roasty Potatoes with Sage, developed by Ruth Lively of Kitchen Garden magazine, is superb with cheese or egg dishes.

Preheat the oven to 425°F.

Scrub and dry the potatoes. Pour the oil into a 12-inch gratin dish, casserole, or large ovenproof skillet. Lay the sage leaves flat on the oiled surface, covering the bottom with a single layer. Sprinkle the salt over the sage.

Cut the potatoes in half and arrange them, cut side down, on the sage leaves. Bake, uncovered, 35-40 minutes, or until the potatoes are tender and the cut sides are crusty brown.

Serves 4

MOROCCAN POTATOES AND PEPPERS

2 tablespoons olive oil

1 teaspoon ground coriander
  seeds

1 teaspoon ground cumin

10 small or medium cloves
  garlic, sliced very thin

3 red or green bell peppers,
  preferably a combination,
  seeded and sliced

1 jalapeño chile, seeded and
  minced

4 medium potatoes, peeled
  and quartered

3 cups hot water

juice and zest of 1 lemon

salt and freshly ground black
  pepper, to taste

Succulent chunks of potato awash in a savory sauce make this a good choice for a brunch accompaniment to an egg dish. Don't be put off by the amount of garlic called for in this recipe. Because the garlic is sliced very thin and then simmered, it adds a rather mysterious soft whisper of flavor that blends easily with the other seasonings.

In a large frying pan, heat the oil over medium heat. When hot, add the coriander, cumin, and garlic. Sauté 1-2 minutes, then stir in the bell and chile peppers. Sauté 3-4 minutes.

Add the potatoes, water, and lemon juice and zest. Season with salt and pepper. Bring to a boil, then lower the heat, partially cover, and simmer 30 minutes. If the sauce has not thickened slightly after 30 minutes, uncover and simmer 5 more minutes. Serve hot.

Serves 4-6

*Moroccan Potatoes and Peppers
(recipe this page)*

FOUR TOPPINGS
FOR BAKED POTATOES

Parsley Pesto
¾ cup hazelnuts
2 cups washed, loosely packed
   Italian parsley leaves
½ teaspoon grated lemon peel
1 tablespoon freshly squeezed
   lemon juice
¼ cup vegetable oil
salt and freshly ground black
   pepper, to taste
1-3 tablespoons water,
   if necessary

Fresh Tomato
and Chipotle Salsa
2 medium tomatoes, finely
   chopped
1 medium onion, finely
   chopped
2 tablespoons chopped
   cilantro
juice of 1 lime
1-3 canned chipotle chiles
salt, to taste

My image of potato perfection is a crisp-skinned baked potato with its tender innards gilded with either butter or sour cream and sprinkled with chives, salt, and freshly ground black pepper. However, every once in a while it's fun to venture off the beaten track. Here, then, are four possibilities for a baked potato escapade. When serving them, you might want to cut the potatoes in half lengthwise to create more of a surface to top. All topping recipes make enough for at least 6 large baked potatoes.

Baked potatoes
6 large baking potatoes

Preheat the oven to 400°F. Prick the potatoes several times with a fork and bake 45-60 minutes, or until tender.

Parsley Pesto

Emerald green and rich with toasted hazelnuts, this pesto is also delicious on pasta, steamed vegetables, and toasted slices of coarse grained bread. Toasting and removing the skins of the hazelnuts give them a finer flavor.

Preheat the oven to 350°F.
   To toast the hazelnuts, place them on a baking sheet and bake 10-15 minutes. To remove their skins, allow them to cool several minutes, then rub them by handfuls in a rough towel. (There may be flecks of skin left on the hazelnuts, which is fine.)

Place the parsley, hazelnuts, lemon peel, and lemon juice in a food processor. Pulse until the parsley is roughly chopped. With the motor running, add the oil slowly and process until a purée is formed. Season with salt and pepper. If the pesto is too stiff, mix in water until the desired consistency is reached.

Serves 6

Fresh Tomato and Chipotle Salsa
Chipotle chiles lend their smoky heat to this fresh salsa, which can range from merely warm to fiery hot, depending upon the number of chiles used. My advice is to start out with one and keep going until the desired amount of gustatory fireworks is reached. Any leftover salsa disappears quickly when served with tortilla chips.

Dill, Mustard, and Yogurt Topping

1¼ cups low-fat plain yogurt

2 scallions, green and white
    parts, finely chopped
    (¼ cup)

3 tablespoons Dijon mustard

2 tablespoons finely chopped
    fresh dill

salt and freshly ground black
    pepper, to taste

Hark Fatootie with Sour Cream

8-10 jalapeño chiles (about
    2 cups)

1 medium onion, peeled and
    quartered

½ large head garlic,
    separated into cloves

2 tablespoons olive oil

¾ teaspoon salt

sour cream, to taste

Place the tomatoes, onions, cilantro, and lime juice in a medium bowl. One at a time, chop each chile, add to the bowl, and stir well. Taste after each addition, stopping when the desired hotness is reached. Season with salt and stir.

Serves 6

Dill, Mustard, and Yogurt Topping

This tasty, low-fat combination enhances any potato and is a snap to prepare. Leftovers make a great topping for steamed vegetables or a dip for crisp, fresh vegetables.

In a small bowl, whisk together the yogurt, scallions, mustard, and dill. Season with salt and pepper. Set aside 1 hour to allow the flavors to marry.

Serves 6

Hark Fatootie with Sour Cream

The cause is long lost to obscurity, but the traditional exclamation when anyone in my family tasted something on the torrid side was "Hark fatootie, that's hot!" This richly flavored combination of roasted jalapeños, garlic, and onions is hot but when cut with

sour cream is transformed into a marvelous blend of hot and cool. For a version with less heat, slice the chiles in half and scrape out the membranes and seeds.

Preheat the oven to 350°F.

Cut the stems off the chiles. Place the chiles, onions, and garlic in a single layer in a medium, shallow baking dish.

Drizzle the vegetables with oil and mix well. Roast 30 minutes. Remove from the oven, and turn the vegetables over with a fork. Return to the oven, and roast another 30 minutes.

Remove the vegetables from the oven and cool slightly. Peel off the papery skin from the garlic. Place the vegetables and the salt in a food processor, and process until completely blended but not overly puréed. Add to sour cream until the desired hotness and flavor is reached. (I find that about ¼ cup of Hark Fatootie to 1 cup sour cream is about right.)

Serves 6

BAKED FRIES

4 medium baking potatoes
2 tablespoons vegetable oil
salt, to taste

*A*nd now, folks, you too can have the taste of french-fried potatoes in the privacy of your own home without resorting to hauling out a deep fryer or a trip to Mickey D's. This method of cooking potatoes is a no-muss, no-fuss way of serving up a delicious plate of fries with a whole lot less fat than the real thing.

Preheat the oven to 450°F.

Peel the potatoes and cut them into french fry-sized strips. Arrange them on a baking sheet in a single layer. Drizzle with the oil and mix thoroughly.

Bake 30-40 minutes, or until golden brown and tender. During baking, remove from the oven every 10 minutes and turn the potatoes with a spatula to ensure even browning. When done, remove from the oven and season with salt. Serve hot.

Serves 4

GREEK POTATOES

6 medium boiling or
    all-purpose potatoes,
    peeled and cut in ¾-inch
    cubes
⅓-½ cup freshly squeezed
    lemon juice (2-2½ lemons)
2 tablespoons vegetable oil
2 tablespoons olive oil
1½ teaspoons dried oregano
2 cloves garlic, minced
2 teaspoons salt
½ teaspoon freshly ground
    black pepper
2 cups hot water

These chunks of roasted potatoes enlivened with lemon, garlic, and oregano are a great local favorite. I know of at least one successful courtship in which Greek Potatoes were used as a lure. The restaurant where this dish originated is gone, but the dish lives on in glory thanks to its publication in New Recipes from Moosewood Restaurant. *In this version, the potatoes are briefly steamed, which shortens the roasting time.*

Preheat the oven to 475°F.

Place the potatoes in a steamer basket over simmering water, cover, and steam 10 minutes. Remove from the steamer and transfer to a 9-inch by 12-inch baking dish.

In the baking dish, combine the potatoes with the lemon juice, oils, oregano, garlic, salt, and pepper. Add the water, and bake 1 hour, or until lightly browned. Check the water level during the last 20 minutes of cooking, adding more if necessary. Serve hot.

Serves 6

INDIAN HOME FRIES

6 medium boiling potatoes
4 tablespoons water
2 tablespoons grated fresh
  ginger
4 cloves garlic, finely chopped
1 teaspoon salt
½ teaspoon turmeric
pinch of ground red pepper
2 tablespoons vegetable oil
1 heaping teaspoon fennel
  seeds

This dish uses an Indian cooking technique that results in mouth-watering spicy potatoes fried to a crisp golden brown. Like American home fries, the potatoes are first cooked until tender before they are sautéed. However, before that final step, they are tossed with a tantalizing paste of garlic, fresh ginger, a bit of turmeric, and ground red pepper, and then fried with whole fennel seed. This dish is marvelous with roast chicken.

In a large pot, cover the potatoes with water and bring to a boil. Lower the heat and simmer, covered, 30-35 minutes, or until tender. Drain, cool slightly, and peel. Cut the potatoes into ½-inch to ¾-inch cubes.

In a blender, process the water, ginger, garlic, salt, turmeric, and red pepper until a paste is formed.

In a large, preferably nonstick frying pan, heat the oil over medium-high heat. When hot, add the fennel and cook 30 seconds. Remove from the heat, stir in the spice paste, then cook 2 minutes. Add the potatoes and stir with a spatula to evenly coat them with the spice paste. Fry 10-15 minutes, turning occasionally, until the potatoes have a golden brown crust.

Serves 4-6

*Indian Home Fries
(recipe this page)*

PAPAS CHORREADAS

8-12 small boiling potatoes,
about 2 inches in diameter
1½ tablespoons olive oil
2 medium onions, chopped
3 cloves garlic, minced
1-2 jalapeño chiles, seeded and
finely chopped
1½ teaspoons turmeric
1 teaspoon ground cumin
1 teaspoon grated fresh
ginger, or ¼ teaspoon dried
one 14-ounce can tomatoes
with juice, chopped
¼ cup minced cilantro
½ pound green beans,
trimmed and snapped into
2-inch lengths
1 cup grated Monterey Jack,
Muenster, or mild Cheddar
cheese
½ cup low-fat sour cream
salt and freshly ground black
pepper, to taste

*T*his very colorful and delectable dish from Colombia makes an attractive offering at a dinner party. A bright golden sauce with flecks of red tomato and green cilantro gilds small white potatoes and bright green snap beans.

Accompanied by halves of hard-boiled eggs, black olives, and tomato wedges, this dish is substantial enough for an entrée. Just add a loaf of crusty bread, a green salad, and top it off with a decadent dessert.

In a large pot, cover the potatoes with water and bring to a boil over high heat. Lower the heat and simmer 20 minutes, or until tender. Drain and cover to keep warm.

While the potatoes are cooking, heat the oil in a large frying pan over medium heat. When hot, add the onions, garlic, and chiles, and cook 4-5 minutes, or until the onions are softened. Stir in the turmeric, cumin, and ginger, and cook 1-2 minutes. Add the tomatoes and cilantro, and simmer over low heat 10 minutes.

Place the green beans in a steamer basket and steam over simmering water 3 minutes, or just until tender. Remove from the heat and mix with the potatoes.

Stir the cheese and sour cream into the tomato mixture and slowly heat until the cheese is melted. Season with salt and pepper.

Place the green bean and potato mixture in a serving bowl and top with the sauce.

Serves 6 as a side dish,
4 as an entrée

Note: To serve this dish as an entrée, arrange plates with lettuce leaves and spoon the green bean and potato mixture on top. Pour the sauce over each serving, and garnish with halves of hard-boiled eggs, wedges of tomato, and black olives.

ACCIDENTAL BAKED AND STUFFED POTATOES

4 medium baking potatoes
4 slices bacon
½ cup chopped scallions,
    green and white parts
1 tablespoon fresh dill, or
    1 teaspoon dried
3 tablespoons cider vinegar
¼ cup sour cream
salt and freshly ground black
    pepper, to taste

The taste of these baked and stuffed potatoes was inspired by my husband's attempt to whomp up a batch of the German Potato Salad that his parents' delicatessen was famous for. The potatoes were inadvertantly overcooked, and the result was an extremely flavorful mashed potato dish. Using the basic tangy flavorings of German Potato Salad and adding a bit of sour cream and dill, I came up with these comforting, overstuffed spuds.

Preheat the oven to 400°F.

Prick each potato several times with a fork and bake 45-60 minutes, or until tender. Remove from the oven and cool.

While the potatoes are baking, place the bacon in a large frying pan and cook over medium heat, turning occasionally, until crisp. Remove and drain on a paper towel, reserving 2 tablespoons of the bacon fat in the pan. With a sharp knife, chop the bacon into small pieces.

Add the scallions and dill to the bacon fat, stir, and cook over medium heat 2-3 minutes.

Slice off the top one-quarter of the potatoes horizontally. With a spoon, scoop out the flesh of the top portion into a medium bowl and discard the top skin. Scoop out the flesh of the remaining portion into the bowl, keeping the skin intact. Mash the potatoes, then add the bacon, scallions, dill, bacon fat, vinegar, and sour cream and stir together. Season with salt and pepper. Spoon this mixture into the potato skins and reheat at 400°F 10 minutes.

Serves 4

Note: A virtue of baked stuffed potatoes is that they can be prepared ahead, refrigerated, and cooked later. Reheat in a microwave, or preheat a conventional oven to 375°F, cover the potatoes loosely with aluminum foil, and heat 20-25 minutes.

Main Dishes

Indian Potato Patties
(recipe on page 126)

INDIAN POTATO PATTIES

3 medium boiling potatoes
⅓ cup minced onions
1½ tablespoons grated fresh
 ginger
1 small jalapeño chile, seeded
 and minced
¾ teaspoon cumin seeds,
 toasted
¼ cup chopped cilantro,
 packed
6 tablespoons dry bread-
 crumbs
2 tablespoons lime juice
½ teaspoon salt
⅛ teaspoon freshly ground
 black pepper
1-2 tablespoons vegetable oil
Mint Cilantro Chutney, 1 recipe

Mint Cilantro Chutney
1 medium green bell pepper,
 roughly chopped
⅓ cup chopped cilantro, lightly
 packed
¼ cup chopped fresh mint,
 lightly packed
½ cup grated, unsweetened
 coconut
¼ cup low-fat plain yogurt
2 tablespoons lemon juice
½ teaspoon salt
½ teaspoon cumin seeds,
 toasted, optional
½ jalapeño chile, minced,
 optional

These zesty little patties are wonderful with a simple chicken or fish entrée or even in the starring entrée role themselves. Although they are marvelous by themselves, I think they are even better when accompanied by a Mint Cilantro Chutney. (Photo on page 124.)

In a medium pot, cover the potatoes with water and bring to a boil over high heat. Lower the heat and simmer 30-35 minutes, or until the potatoes are tender. Drain and cool slightly.

In a large bowl, mash the potatoes using a potato masher or ricer. Stir in the onions, ginger, chiles, cumin, cilantro, breadcrumbs, lime juice, salt, and pepper and mix thoroughly. Let stand 15 minutes.

Shape the potato mixture into small patties, about 2 inches in diameter and ½ inch thick. In a large nonstick or heavy frying pan, heat the oil over medium heat. When hot, add the patties and sauté 3-4 minutes on each side, or until browned.

Serve hot, accompanied by the Mint Cilantro Chutney.

Yields ten 2-inch patties

Mint Cilantro Chutney

Combine the ingredients in a food processor or blender. Process 1 minute, or until the mixture is pulverized but not liquified.

POTATO SOUFFLÉ

3 medium potatoes
2 tablespoons butter
½ cup low-fat cottage cheese
3 large eggs, separated
1 scallion, green and white
   parts, minced
1 teaspoon salt
¼-½ teaspoon freshly ground
   black pepper
¼ teaspoon cream of tartar

*T*his elegant entrée, with its golden brown top, is wonderfully smooth and light. Steamed, minted carrots and broccoli braised in a drizzle of olive oil and lemon juice are nice accompaniments.

In a medium pot, cover the potatoes with water and bring to a boil over high heat. Lower the heat and simmer 30-45 minutes, or until tender.

Preheat the oven to 400°F.

Drain, peel, and cut the potatoes into chunks. In a large bowl or food processor, combine the potatoes, butter, cottage cheese, and egg yolks and mash or purée until smooth. Mix in the scallions, salt, and pepper.

In a small, deep bowl or 4-cup measure, beat the egg whites with the cream of tartar until stiff. Gently fold the egg whites into the potato mixture.

Spoon into a greased 6-cup soufflé dish or straight-sided casserole. Bake 25-30 minutes, or until the soufflé has risen and the top is golden brown. Serve hot.

Serves 4

POTATO-BROCCOLI PIE

1 unbaked 9-inch pie shell
6-8 small boiling potatoes,
about 2 inches in diameter
1½ tablespoons olive oil
1 medium stalk broccoli,
peeled and chopped
1 medium onion, chopped
2 cloves garlic, minced
½ teaspoon dried basil
salt and freshly ground black
pepper, to taste
1 cup freshly grated Parmesan
cheese
3 large eggs
¾ cup milk
1 teaspoon Dijon mustard

This delicious pie is a layer of herbed broccoli and onions sandwiched between succulent potatoes and Parmesan cheese. The top bakes to a satisfying crustiness, and the whole is complemented by an accompaniment of airy, puréed carrots and a crisp green salad.

Prepare the pie shell or thaw if frozen.

In a medium pot, cover the potatoes with water and bring to a boil over high heat. Lower the heat and simmer, covered, 15-20 minutes, or until tender. Remove from the heat and drain. Allow the potatoes to cool slightly, then peel and thinly slice them.

Preheat the oven to 350°F.

In a large nonstick frying pan, heat the oil over medium-high heat. When hot, add the broccoli, onions, garlic, and basil. Cook, stirring occasionally, until the onions begin to brown. Remove from the heat and season with salt and pepper.

Place a thin layer of sliced potatoes in the bottom of the pie shell. Sprinkle with salt, pepper, and ⅓ cup of the cheese. Add the broccoli mixture, and top with a single layer of potatoes, overlapping them in concentric rings. Sprinkle with salt, pepper, and ⅓ cup of the cheese.

In a small bowl or food processor, beat the eggs, milk, and mustard until well blended. Carefully pour over the pie, then top with the remaining cheese. Place the pie on a baking sheet and bake 1 hour. Allow the pie to set 15 minutes. Cut into wedges and serve hot.

Serves 4-6

*Potato-Broccoli Pie
(recipe this page)*

POTATO ROLL-UPS
WITH ONION CHUTNEY

6 medium boiling potatoes, peeled and cut into ½-inch cubes

2 scallions, green and white parts, chopped

1-2 jalapeño chiles, seeded and minced

¼ cup chopped cilantro

½ teaspoon turmeric

½ teaspoon ground cumin

1¼ cups low-fat plain yogurt

salt and freshly ground black pepper, to taste

eight 7-inch flour tortillas

Onion Chutney

1 medium onion, chopped

½ teaspoon sweet paprika

½ teaspoon salt

1½ tablespoons lemon juice

pinch of ground red pepper

I suppose this quick and easy dish could be classified as "fusion cooking." With Mexican flour tortillas enclosing a potato filling sparked by Indian seasonings, this recipe is clearly an East-West hybrid. A chutney, either a commercial mango or this fresh onion one, enhances this dish. I like to serve these roll-ups with lentils cooked with lemons and browned onions as well as a crisp, garden salad.

Steam the potatoes over boiling water 20 minutes, or until tender. Transfer them to a large bowl, and mix in the scallions, chiles, cilantro, turmeric, cumin, and yogurt. Season with salt and pepper, and stir to combine thoroughly.

Preheat the oven to 300°F.

Place some of the mixture in the center of each tortilla and roll the tortilla around it. Arrange the tortillas in a shallow baking dish and heat 10-15 minutes. Serve hot, accompanied by the Onion Chutney.

Serves 4-6

Onion Chutney

In a small bowl, combine the onions, paprika, salt, lemon juice, and red pepper. Set aside 1 hour to allow the flavors to mellow.

SAVORY POTATO CALZONES

Dough

1 package dry yeast
   (2½ teaspoons)
1¼ cups warm water
1 teaspoon sugar
1½ teaspoons salt
3 cups white bread flour or
   all-purpose flour
1 tablespoon olive oil

Filling

1½ tablespoons olive oil
1 medium onion, finely
   chopped
2 cloves garlic, minced
¾ teaspoon dried basil
4 medium boiling potatoes, cut
   into ¼-inch cubes
2 tablespoons drained capers,
   rinsed
¾ teaspoon salt
½ teaspoon freshly ground
   black pepper
⅔ cup water
¾ cup of ½-inch fontina cheese
   cubes

Calzones are highly portable turnovers that are perfect out-of-hand food for a picnic or a casual buffet dinner. These calzones feature a potato and creamy fontina cheese filling sparked with the zing of capers. Capers, which are the pickled floral buds of a Mediterranean shrub, add a tantalizing tart-salty note to the filling. I like to freeze left-over calzones and reheat them 20-30 minutes at 400°F.

For the dough, dissolve the yeast in ½ cup of the water in a large, warmed bowl. Add the sugar and set aside 10 minutes. Add the remaining water. In a small bowl, mix the salt with the flour and gradually add to the liquid. Stir the mixture until it is stiff, then knead it briefly in the bowl, adding the olive oil. Turn out onto a floured surface and knead 5 minutes, or until the dough is smooth and elastic. Form the dough into a ball, return it to the bowl, and cover. Allow the dough to rise in a warm place 1 hour, or until it has doubled in size.

For the filling, in a large frying pan with a cover, heat the oil over medium-high heat. Sauté the onions, garlic, and basil 3-4 minutes. Add the potatoes, capers, salt, pepper, and water. Over high heat, bring to a boil. Lower the heat, cover, and simmer 15-20 minutes, or until the potatoes are tender.

To assemble, punch down the dough and place it on a large, lightly floured surface. Form it into a 10-inch cylinder, then with a sharp knife, cut the cylinder into 10 equal portions. Press or roll each portion into a 2-inch to 3-inch circle. Cover with a dish towel and let rest 10 minutes.

Preheat the oven to 425°F.

Using a floured rolling pin, roll each dough portion into a 6-inch circle.

Add the cheese to the potato mixture. Place ¼-⅓ cup of the filling on one half of a dough circle. With a pastry brush, brush a strip of water along ½ inch of the inside bottom edge. Fold the other half over the filling. With your fingers, press the edges together to seal. The edges will have a dimpled look. Place on an ungreased baking sheet.

Continue in this manner until all of the calzones are filled. Bake 15 minutes. Remove the calzones from the baking sheets and cool on wire racks. Serve hot.

Yields 10

TORTILLA ESPAÑOLA
WITH ROMESCO

1½ tablespoons olive oil
2 medium onions, thinly sliced
2 medium-large potatoes,
    peeled, halved lengthwise,
    and thinly sliced
salt and freshly ground black
    pepper, to taste
6 eggs

Romesco
1 tablespoon olive oil
1 slice coarse textured bread
¼ cup whole unblanched
    almonds
¼ cup canned or fresh toma-
    toes, chopped
¼ cup canned or fresh red bell
    peppers, chopped
1-2 cloves garlic, minced
¼ teaspoon paprika
2 tablespoons wine vinegar
¼ cup extra-virgin olive oil
salt and freshly ground black
    pepper, to taste

In Spain, tortilla has a different meaning from the circular flattened corn- or wheat-flour wrappers that we are used to. A Spanish tortilla is a frittata-like omelet, and the classic example of this, tortilla española, is made with potatoes. Romesco, native to Catalonia, is a sauce with an intriguing combination of toasted almonds, grilled bread, garlic, tomatoes, and red peppers. It is addictive on grilled food, as well as on baked potatoes. I recommend allowing the sauce to rest at room temperature for 3 to 4 hours to let the flavors mellow.

In a 10-inch nonstick frying pan, heat the oil over medium-high heat. Add the onions and potatoes, and stir to coat with oil. Cook 15-20 minutes, or until the potatoes are tender and the onions are slightly browned. Spread the onions and potatoes into an even layer, and season with salt and pepper.

In a medium bowl, whisk or beat the eggs and salt until thoroughly combined. Pour over the potato and onion mixture, and reduce the heat to low. Cook 10-15 minutes, or until the omelet is firm.

Loosen the edges of the omelet from the pan, then transfer to a large plate in one of two ways: by inverting the plate over the frying pan, holding both together, and flipping the omelet onto the plate, or by holding the frying pan next to the plate and sliding the omelet onto it. Transfer the omelet back to the frying pan with the uncooked side down. Cook 3-4 minutes.

Cut into quarters and serve hot along with the Romesco.

Serves 4

Romesco

In a small frying pan, heat the oil over medium heat. When hot, sauté the bread until golden on both sides. Remove from the heat and cut into 1-inch pieces.

Heat a skillet, then toast the almonds, turning often, 10 minutes.

In a food processor or blender, grind the almonds until fine. Add the bread, tomatoes, peppers, garlic, paprika, and vinegar, and process until the mixture becomes a smooth paste. With the motor running, add the extra-virgin olive oil in a thin stream. Season with salt and pepper.

*Tortilla Española with Romesco
(recipe this page)*

POTATO BURGERS WITH
SMOKED CHEDDAR AND SCALLIONS

8 medium all-purpose or
  boiling potatoes

4-5 scallions, green and white
  parts, minced (⅔ cup)

1 teaspoon salt

½ teaspoon freshly ground
  black pepper

1 egg

3 tablespoons low-fat sour
  cream

½ cup heaped, coarsely grated
  smoked Cheddar cheese

1 tablespoon vegetable oil

Although sautéed meat or vegetable patties can be had around the world, "burgers" conjures up a distinctly American image. I once had a friend who delighted in making burgers out of various non-traditional ingredients—beetburgers were her most notorious attempt in this area. These tasty burgers are always popular. Try serving them topped with a juicy red slab of fresh tomato when good ones are available in the summer.

In a large pot, cover the potatoes with water and bring to a boil. Lower the heat and simmer 15-20 minutes, or until the potatoes are slightly cooked but still firm. Drain and cool slightly. Peel and grate the potatoes into a large bowl using a food processor or the largest holes on a metal grater. Add the scallions, salt, and pepper to the potatoes and mix to combine.

In a small bowl, whisk the egg and sour cream together. Add to the potatoes, then stir in the cheese. Form the mixture into patties approximately 3½ inches in diameter and ¾ inch thick.

In a large frying pan, heat half of the oil over medium heat. When hot, add half of the patties and cook about 4 minutes, or until crisp and brown on the bottom. Flip the patties over with a spatula and cook another 4 minutes. Repeat with the remaining oil and patties. Serve hot.

Yields eight 3½-inch patties

Potato Gnocchi with Sun-Dried Tomato and Fresh Basil Sauce (recipe on pages 136-137)

POTATO GNOCCHI WITH SUN-DRIED TOMATO AND FRESH BASIL SAUCE

3 large baking potatoes
¼ cup milk
1 large egg, beaten
salt and freshly ground black
    pepper, to taste
½-1 cup flour
Sun-Dried Tomato and Fresh
    Basil Sauce, 1 recipe
½-¾ cup freshly grated
    Parmesan cheese

**Sun-Dried Tomato
and Fresh Basil Sauce**
¾ cup sun-dried tomatoes
    (approximately 16 halves)
1 cup boiling water
½ cup roughly chopped basil
1 clove garlic, minced
2 tablespoons olive oil
2 tablespoons dry white wine
1 tablespoon balsamic vinegar
salt and freshly ground black
    pepper, to taste

In this luscious dish, succulent potato dumplings repose on a layer of zesty and easily made sauce and are crowned with crusty, browned Parmesan cheese. A fresh green salad, some Italian bread, and a dry red wine make this a memorable meal. (Photo on page 135.)

In a medium pot, cover the potatoes with water and bring to a boil over high heat. Lower the heat and simmer, partially covered, 30-45 minutes, or until tender. Drain, cool, and peel the potatoes. Cut the potatoes into chunks, then put them through a ricer or the fine disc of a food mill into a large bowl.

Stir in the milk and egg and season liberally with salt and pepper. Stir in ½ cup of the flour and blend thoroughly. Spread some of the remaining flour on a bread board. Turn out the potato mixture onto the board and work just enough of the flour to make a dough that is soft yet firm enough to hold its shape when the gnocchi are formed. (The less flour used, the more tender the gnocchi will be.)

Divide the dough into quarters, then roll each one into a cylinder with a ¾-inch to 1-inch diameter. Place the cylinders on a floured platter or baking sheet and refrigerate 30 minutes.

To form the gnocchi, line up the cylinders of dough 4 abreast. With a long, sharp knife, slice through all the cylinders, cutting them into ½-inch pieces. Spread the slices on a floured surface and let dry 10 minutes.

To cook the gnocchi, use a spatula to scoop up several and drop them into a large soup pot of boiling salted water. Cook only as many as will fit in a single layer on the bottom of the pot. When the water returns to a boil, reduce the heat to a simmer. When the gnocchi bob to the surface, simmer gently 5 minutes.

While the gnocchi are cooking, spread the bottom of a large, shallow baking dish with a layer of hot Sun-Dried Tomato and Fresh Basil Sauce. Remove the gnocchi from the pot with a slotted spoon, and place them in a single layer in the baking dish. Repeat this process until all the gnocchi have been cooked, starting each time with boiling water. Sprinkle the gnocchi with the cheese and place under a broiler until hot and browned. Serve immediately.

Serves 4-6

Note: Because gnocchi are delicate dumplings, it is important that the water remain at a simmer, not a boil, when they are cooking so they don't begin to disintegrate.

Sun-Dried Tomato and Fresh Basil Sauce

Place the tomatoes in a small bowl and pour the water over them. Let stand 30 minutes. Inspect the tomatoes for tough stem scars and remove with scissors, if necessary. In a blender or food processor, purée the tomatoes, water, basil, garlic, oil, white wine, vinegar, salt, and pepper until smooth.

POTATO AND BACON PIZZA

Crust
1 package yeast
    (2½ teaspoons)
1¼ cups warm water
1 teaspoon sugar
1 tablespoon olive oil
3 cups white bread flour or
    all-purpose flour
1½ teaspoons salt

Topping
8 slices bacon
5-6 medium potatoes
3½ tablespoons olive oil
3 medium cloves garlic, minced
2 teaspooons minced fresh
    rosemary
2 cups grated sharp Cheddar
    cheese
salt and freshly ground black
    pepper, to taste
1 cup freshly grated Parmesan
    cheese

*W*hile striving to lead a low-fat life, every once in a while I yearn for an oleaginous blowout. This pizza has a prime ingredient of dietary sin: bacon. Actually, the bacon is an indulgence; this pizza still tastes great without it. If you don't want to go to the trouble of cooking bacon, you can strew thinly sliced pepperoni over the top.*

For the crust, dissolve the yeast in ½ cup of the water in a large, warmed bowl. Add the sugar and set aside 10 minutes. Add the remaining water and the oil. In a small bowl, mix the flour and salt, then gradually add to the liquid. Stir the mixture until it is stiff, then knead it briefly in the bowl.

Turn the dough out onto a floured surface and knead 5 minutes, or until the dough is smooth and elastic. Form the dough into a ball. Clean and oil the bowl, then return the dough to it and cover. Allow the dough to rise in a warm place 1 hour, or until it has doubled in size.

Punch the dough down, divide it in half, and form the two halves into balls. Place the balls on a large, lightly floured surface, and press them with your hands into 6-inch to 7-inch circles. Cover with a dish towel and let rest 10 minutes. With a rolling pin, roll into larger circles of about 12 inches. Place the dough on 12-inch pizza pans or baking sheets and allow to rest.

Preheat the oven to 425°F.

For the topping, in a large frying pan over medium-low heat, cook the bacon 10 minutes, or until it begins to brown. Drain the bacon on paper towels, then chop into bits.

Slice the unpeeled potatoes 1⁄16 inch thick. In a small bowl, mix the oil, garlic, and rosemary.

To assemble, sprinkle each crust with 1 cup of the Cheddar. Starting ½ inch from the outside of the crust and using the largest potato slices, overlap the slices in concentric rings until the surface is covered. Save the smaller slices for center rings.

With a spoon, drizzle the oil mixture over the potatoes. Season with salt and pepper. Divide the bacon pieces in half and distribute evenly over the potatoes. Sprinkle ½ cup of the Parmesan over each pizza. Bake 15-20 minutes. Serve hot.

Yields two 12-inch pizzas

Potato and Bacon Pizza
(recipe this page)

POTATO TURNOVERS
WITH GARLICKY GREENS FILLING

Turnovers

4 medium baking potatoes, or
   2½ cups unseasoned
   mashed potatoes made
   with baking potatoes

1 cup flour (preferably half
   whole wheat)

½ teaspoon baking powder

2 tablespoons butter, melted

2 eggs, beaten

½ cup freshly grated Parmesan
   cheese

salt and freshly ground black
   pepper, to taste

Filling

6-7 cups washed and packed
   cooking greens (spinach,
   chard, kale, oriental greens,
   broccoli raab, dandelion,
   turnip, mustard, or beet
   greens)

2 tablespoons olive oil

1 medium onion, chopped

3 cloves garlic, minced

salt and freshly ground black
   pepper, to taste

*T*his recipe is a prime example of the versatility of taters. In this dish, mashed potatoes are transformed into soft dough squares folded and wrapped around tangy cooked greens, then baked to a golden finish.

For the turnovers, in a large pot, cover the potatoes with water and bring to a boil over high heat. Lower the heat and simmer, covered, 30-35 minutes, or until tender. Drain, cool slightly, and peel the potatoes.

In a small bowl, mix the flour and baking powder and set aside. In a large bowl, rice or mash the potatoes to equal 2½ cups. Add the flour mixture, butter, eggs, and cheese. Season with salt and pepper and mix thoroughly. Chill at least 1 hour.

For the filling, in a large pot, bring 1 inch of water to a boil. Add the greens and steam 1-2 minutes, or until just wilted. Remove from the heat and drain. Squeeze the greens well to remove excess liquid, then transfer to a chopping block and chop roughly.

In a large frying pan, heat the oil over medium-high heat. When hot, add the onions and cook, stirring occasionally, until slightly browned. Add the garlic and cook 1 minute. Add the greens, season with salt and pepper, and mix well. Cook 1-2 minutes, then remove from the heat.

Preheat the oven to 450°F.

To assemble, turn out the dough onto a well-floured surface with a rubber spatula. The dough will be soft. With your hands, form and pat the dough into a rectangle approximately 5 inches by 7 inches. With a well-floured rolling pin, form the dough into a 10-inch by 15-inch rectangle that is about ¼ inch thick. You may have to trim the sides and add to the corners to get a rectangle. With a knife, divide the dough in half vertically and into thirds horizontally. (The result should be six 5-inch squares that will be folded in half diagonally to form triangles.)

Place a heaping tablespoon of the filling on the left-hand side of an imaginary line stretching diagonally from corner to corner of the dough square. Spread the filling to within ½ inch of the edge. Gently flip the unfilled half of the dough over the filling so that the top and bottom edges meet. With your fingertips, press the edges together to seal, forming a dimpled pattern. With a spatula, transfer to a large oiled baking sheet. Repeat with the remaining squares.

Bake 18-20 minutes, or until browned. Serve warm.

Yields 6

Note: I like to mix various greens for this filling and try to balance the mild ones, such as spinach, beet greens, or kale, with the stronger flavors of dandelion greens, turnip greens, or broccoli raab.

POTATO-STUFFED POBLANO CHILES WITH FRESH TOMATO SALSA

4 medium poblano chiles
1 tablespoon olive oil
1 teaspoon cumin seeds
1 small onion, chopped (⅓ cup)
1 large clove garlic, minced
2 medium boiling potatoes,
    peeled and cut into ¼-inch
    cubes (2½ cups)
1 tablespoon water
2 tablespoons chopped
    cilantro
1 cup grated Monterey Jack
    cheese
salt and freshly ground black
    pepper, to taste
Fresh Tomato Salsa, 1 recipe

Fresh Tomato Salsa
2 medium tomatoes, chopped
1 small onion, finely chopped
1 tablespoon chopped cilantro
1 jalapeño chile, seeded and
    minced
½ cup orange juice
2 tablespoons lemon juice
salt and freshly ground black
    pepper, to taste

Poblanos are tapered, deep forest green chiles, sweetly aromatic and fine tasting with a whisper of heat. This heat dissipates in parboiling, but it's still a good idea to wear gloves when you prepare poblanos. Dried poblanos are known as ancho chiles. Cornbread and beans are a nice accompaniment to this tasty southwestern dish.

Cut the chiles in half lengthwise, leaving the stems intact. With a sharp paring knife, remove the seeds and membranes.

Place the chiles in a large pot of boiling water. Reduce the heat, cover, and simmer 5-10 minutes, or until tender but not soft. Remove the chiles with tongs and arrange them in a baking dish or on a 12-inch pizza pan.

Preheat the oven to 400°F.

In a large nonstick frying pan, heat the oil over medium-high heat. When hot, add the cumin, onions, and garlic, and cook 1-2 minutes. Add the potatoes and water. Cover and cook, stirring occasionally, about 10 minutes, or until the potatoes are nearly tender.

Uncover and cook over high heat until the potatoes are slightly browned. Remove from the heat and stir in the cilantro and cheese. Season with salt and pepper.

Divide the stuffing into 8 portions and spoon into the chiles. Cover with aluminum foil and bake 10 minutes, or until thoroughly heated. Remove the foil, then serve with the Fresh Tomato Salsa.

Serves 4

Fresh Tomato Salsa

In a medium bowl, combine the tomatoes, onions, cilantro, chiles, orange juice, and lemon juice. Season with salt and pepper.

POTATO AND CORN ENCHILADAS WITH SALSA VERDE

3 medium boiling potatoes, cut
    into ¼-inch to ½-inch cubes
1 tablespoon vegetable oil
1 large onion, chopped
    (1½ cups)
1 large jalapeño chile, seeded
    and minced
1 large clove garlic, minced
2 teaspoons ground cumin
2 teaspoons ground coriander
    seeds
1½ cups fresh or frozen corn
    kernels
one 15-ounce can black beans,
    drained
juice of 1 lime
1 tablespoon cilantro, minced
2 cups Salsa Verde
1½ cups grated Cheddar
    cheese
salt and freshly ground black
    pepper, to taste
twelve 6-inch corn torillas

Salsa Verde
20 tomatillos
2-3 fresh jalapeño chiles,
    halved and seeded
1 medium onion, quartered
1 clove garlic, minced
2 tablespoons fresh cilantro,
    minced
2 tablespoons vegetable oil
salt and freshly ground black
    pepper, to taste

As anyone who has grown them can tell you, tomatillo plants are excessively productive. In an effort to keep up with their output, every summer I make and freeze vast amounts of Salsa Verde. And in order to use those vast amounts, I have to venture beyond chips and dip. Here is a dish I invented to decrease the Salsa Verde inventory. It can be assembled ahead of time and heated just before serving.

Place the potatoes in a steamer basket and steam over simmering water 10 minutes, or until tender.

In a large frying pan, heat the oil over medium heat. Add the onions and chiles, and sauté 5-10 minutes, or until the onions begin to brown. Stir in the garlic, cumin, and coriander, and sauté 1-2 minutes. Stir in the corn, beans, potatoes, lime juice, cilantro, ½ cup of the Salsa Verde, and ½ cup of the cheese. Season with salt and pepper.

To soften the tortillas for filling, heat a heavy-bottomed frying pan over medium-high heat. When hot, place individual tortillas in the pan and heat each side 5-10 seconds, or until pliable.

Preheat the oven to 350°F.

Pour about ½ cup of the Salsa Verde into a shallow baking dish that is large enough to hold a single layer of 12 rolled tortillas.

Fill the middle of each tortilla with a strip of filling, then roll the tortilla around the filling. Place the rolled tortillas in the baking dish,

sprinkle with the remaining cheese, and cover with foil. Heat in the oven 15 minutes.

Warm the remaining Salsa Verde in a small saucepan over medium heat. Remove the foil from the enchiladas and serve hot with the extra salsa on the side.

Serves 6

Salsa Verde

Husk and wash the tomatillos, then in a medium pot, boil them in a small amount of water until tender, about 5 minutes.

In a food processor or blender, coarsely chop the chiles and onions. Add the garlic, cilantro, and tomatillos, and process briefly until just blended.

Heat the oil in a large frying pan or saucepan over medium heat. Add the ingredients and cook, stirring occasionally, 5-10 minutes. Cool slightly and serve.

Yields 3-4 cups

BOWTIES WITH CRUSTY POTATO CUBES, FRESH TOMATOES, AND BASIL

3 medium boiling potatoes
1 cup packed basil leaves
3 cloves garlic, minced
6 tablespoons olive oil
4 medium ripe tomatoes, or
    8 plum tomatoes, diced
1 jalapeño chile, seeded and
    minced, or 1 teaspoon red
    pepper flakes
salt and freshly ground black
    pepper, to taste
1 pound bowtie pasta
freshly grated Parmesan
    cheese, to taste

Combining potatoes and pasta can be a difficult assignment; these two starches tend to cancel out each other. In this recipe, adapted from one in Verduras *by Viana La Place, the slippery succulence of the cooked bowties is beautifully complemented by the crisp, small cubes of potato, and both are enveloped in the supreme combination of summer ripe tomatoes and a rustic pesto.*

Steam the potatoes 15-20 minutes, or until tender. Allow the potatoes to cool slightly, then peel and dice them.

While the potatoes are cooking, combine the basil, garlic, and 4 tablespoons of the oil in a blender or food processor. Purée until a rough pesto forms.

In a medium bowl, combine the tomatoes, chiles, and pesto. Season with salt and pepper, mash lightly with a fork, and set aside.

Over high heat, put a large pot of water on to boil for the pasta. Preheat the broiler.

In another medium bowl, toss the potatoes with the remaining oil. Spread the potatoes on a broiler tray, and season with salt and pepper. Broil, turning occasionally, until the potatoes have a golden brown crust.

Cook the pasta according to the package instructions and drain. Stir the potatoes into the tomato mixture. Divide the pasta among warmed, shallow bowls and top with the potato mixture. Sprinkle each serving with Parmesan cheese and serve immediately.

Serves 6-8

Bowties with Crusty Potato Cubes, Fresh Tomatoes, and Basil (recipe this page)

NEW POTATOES
WITH BLACK BEANS AND SHRIMP

6 small new potatoes
(1½ pounds)
½ cup olive oil
juice of 1 lemon (3 tablespoons)
1 tablespoon balsamic vinegar
½-¾ cup chopped scallions,
green and white parts
1 tablespoon minced fresh
cilantro
1 tablespoon minced fresh
basil
salt and freshly ground black
pepper, to taste
2 cups black beans, rinsed and
drained (one 15-ounce can)
1 large tomato, chopped
1 pound shelled, cleaned
medium shrimp
lemon slices or wedges,
garnish

This is a delightful dish to try when the new crop of small red potatoes is in the market or ready in your garden. It's a pretty concoction that looks lovely when served in pasta bowls with a bright green tossed salad on the side. If new potatoes are unavailable, this dish is still delicious if you substitute medium boiling potatoes and quarter them.

In a medium pot, cover the potatoes with water and bring to a boil over high heat. Lower the heat, cover, and simmer 20 minutes, or until tender. Remove from the heat, drain, and set aside.

Prepare the dressing by whisking together in a blender or small bowl the oil, lemon juice, vinegar, scallions, cilantro, and basil. Season with salt and pepper.

Cut the potatoes in halves or quarters and place them in a large saucepan. Add the beans, tomatoes, and two-thirds of the dressing. Stir gently to combine, and heat over a low flame.

While the potato mixture is heating, pour the remaining dressing into a large frying pan. Over medium-high heat, cook the shrimp until they are opaque.

To serve, spoon the potato mixture into pasta dishes, and with a slotted spoon, divide the shrimp equally on top. Garnish with lemon slices or wedges.

Serves 4-6

Note: If you have leftovers, store the shrimp and potato mixture in separate containers. The shrimp have a strong flavor that tends to permeate the mixture if left with it too long.

FRITTATA À LA TIM

2 tablespoons olive oil
1 large onion, sliced thin
1 large red bell pepper,
 seeded and sliced thin
 vertically
1 large green bell pepper,
 seeded and sliced thin
 vertically
2 large cloves garlic, minced
1¼ teaspoons dried oregano
2 medium boiling or
 all-purpose potatoes
6 eggs
1 cup milk
salt and freshly ground black
 pepper, to taste
¼ cup pitted and sliced
 kalamata olives
¾-1 cup crumbled feta cheese

If you're crossing the country by bicycle, as my visiting friend Tim was when I made this, accompany this tasty concoction with a carbo load of four pieces of toast. For a leisurely weekend breakfast for ordinary mortals, an accompaniment of fresh fruit, a great cup of coffee, and maybe one or two slices of toast starts the day off right. This layered assemblage of caramelized onions and bell peppers, kalamata olives, sliced potatoes, eggs, and feta cheese also makes a lovely light entrée served with tangy coleslaw.

In a 9-inch frying pan with an ovenproof handle, heat the oil over medium-high heat. When hot, add the onions, peppers, garlic, and oregano. Sauté, stirring frequently, 7-8 minutes, or until the onions and peppers are limp. Lower the heat, and cook slowly 10-15 minutes, or until the onions begin to brown.

Preheat the oven to 375°F.

While the onions and peppers are cooking, peel the potatoes and slice them thin. Place them in the basket of a steamer, and steam 5-10 minutes, or until tender.

In a small bowl, whisk together the eggs and milk. Season with salt and pepper.

Turn the heat up to medium-high under the frying pan. (The pan needs to be hot enough so that the eggs sizzle when they are put in.)

Sprinkle the olives over the vegetables. Add the potatoes in an even layer and season lightly with salt and pepper. Pour in the egg and milk mixture, and top with the cheese.

Lower the heat and cook 2-3 minutes, or until the sides of the egg mixture begin to set and the mixture is warmed. Transfer the pan to the oven and cook 20-25 minutes, or until the eggs are set in the middle. Let stand 5 minutes.

Gently loosen the edges of the frittata with a rubber spatula and cut into wedges. Serve warm.

Serves 6

GATEAU DES POMMES DE TERRE

2 medium russet potatoes
½ cup sun-dried tomatoes
1 cup boiling water
2 tablespoons olive oil
1 medium leek, well rinsed and
    chopped (1 cup)
1¼ teaspoons ground cumin
9½-inch by 10-inch sheet of
    frozen puff pastry
salt and freshly ground black
    pepper, to taste

Only a French name will do for this most elegant of vegetarian entrées. I love the contrast of layers of flaky, crisp puff pastry with the flavorful succulence of potatoes mashed with sun-dried tomatoes and leeks. Frozen puff pastry makes this dish a snap to prepare. Cut into small servings, this dish can be transformed into an appetizer. This gateau makes a lovely presentation on a small serving platter when surrounded by steamed broccoli with lemon butter drizzled over it.

In a medium pot, cover the potatoes with water and bring to a boil over high heat. Lower the heat and simmer, covered, 35-40 minutes, or until tender. Remove the potatoes from the heat, then drain, peel, and cut them into chunks.

While the potatoes are cooking, place the tomatoes in a small bowl and pour the water over them. Let stand 30 minutes, then remove any tough stem scars from the tomatoes with scissors, if necessary. Chop the tomatoes into small pieces and reserve the soaking liquid.

In a medium frying pan, heat the oil over low heat. When hot, add the leeks and cumin and cook slowly 10 minutes.

Preheat the oven to 400°F or the temperature indicated on the puff pastry package. Remove one sheet of the puff pastry from the freezer and thaw at room temperature 30 minutes.

Rice the potatoes into a medium bowl. Add the tomatoes, leeks, and any oil left in the pan. Season with salt and pepper. Mix well with a potato masher or wooden spoon, and add ¼-½ cup of the soaking liquid for a firm but creamy texture.

Gently unroll the pastry so that it lies flat. If the pastry cracks, repair it by brushing it with water and smoothing it over. With a sharp knife, cut the pastry in half.

With a large spoon, place the potato mixture on one of the pastry halves, spreading it evenly. Turn the other pastry half to the side that doesn't show the fold marks and prick it with a fork three or four times, then place it on top of the potato filling.

Transfer the gateau to a baking sheet and bake 30 minutes, or until golden brown. Serve warm.

Serves 4

Gateau des Pommes de Terre (recipe this page)

CUMIN MEATBALLS AND FINGERLING POTATOES IN A TOMATO-CHIPOTLE SAUCE

Meatballs
1 tablespoon vegetable oil
1½ tablespoons cumin seeds
1 medium onion, finely
    chopped (1 cup)
2 cloves garlic, minced
1 pound ground round
1 cup fresh breadcrumbs
1 egg, beaten
½ cup milk
1 teaspoon salt

Sauce
1½ tablespoons olive oil
1 large onion, chopped
    (1½ cups)
one 28-ounce can crushed
    tomatoes
1-2 canned chipotle chiles,
    minced
½ cup water
salt and freshly ground black
    pepper, to taste

8 small fingerling potatoes, or
    4 long, thin boiling pota-
    toes, quartered lengthwise

Here is a savory entrée to warm up a cool autumn evening. It is delicious with corn, in either bread or kernel form.

For the meatballs, in a medium non-stick frying pan, heat the oil over medium-high heat. When hot, add the cumin and cook about 1 minute, or until toasted. Add the onions and garlic and cook 5 minutes, or until the onions are slightly browned.

Scrape the contents of the pan into a large bowl, then add the ground round, breadcrumbs, egg, milk, and salt. Mix well (the mixture will be wet) and form into balls 1½ inches in diameter. Brown over medium-high heat on all sides in small batches in the frying pan.

For the sauce, in a large, heavy-bottomed pot, heat the oil over medium heat. When hot, add the onions and sauté 5 minutes, or until slightly browned. Add the tomatoes, chiles, water, and meatballs, and season with salt and pepper. Bring to a boil, lower the heat, and simmer gently, partially covered, 30 minutes. Stir occasionally to prevent sticking.

Place the potatoes in a steamer basket over simmering water. Cover and steam 20-30 minutes, or until tender. Add the potatoes to the meatballs and sauce. Serve hot.

Serves 6

POTATO, CHICKEN, AND PEA SALAD IN A CITRUS TARRAGON VINAIGRETTE

4 medium boiling potatoes, or
    4 cups tiny new potatoes,
    1 inch to 1½ inches in
    diameter
1 clove garlic, minced
1 teaspoon grated fresh ginger
1 teaspoon grated orange peel
1 tablespoon soy sauce
½ cup water
1 skinless, boneless breast of
    chicken
2 cups shelled peas
Citrus Tarragon Vinaigrette,
    1 recipe
salt and freshly ground black
    pepper, to taste

Citrus Tarragon Vinaigrette
3 tablespoons olive oil
3 tablespoons vegetable oil
¼ cup lemon juice
2 tablespoons white wine
    vinegar
2 teaspoons grated fresh
    ginger
2 teaspoons grated orange
    peel
2 teaspoons dried tarragon

If you can get fresh peas and tiny new potatoes, this main dish salad is a celebration of early summer. The chicken is steamed over a wonderfully aromatic liquid that imparts an orangey-ginger flavor to it. Try this dish with a crisp cucumber salad and steamed artichokes with garlic butter for an elegant meal.

In a medium pot, cover the potatoes with water and bring to a boil over high heat. Lower the heat, cover, and simmer until tender, 25-30 minutes for medium potatoes and 15-20 minutes for new potatoes. Remove from the heat and drain. Peel and cut the medium potatoes into ½-inch to ¾-inch cubes. If using new potatoes, leave the smaller ones whole and cut the larger ones in half. Transfer to a large bowl.

In a medium saucepan, combine the garlic, ginger, orange peel, soy sauce, and water for use as a steaming liquid. Place the chicken in a steamer basket and steam 25 minutes, or until completely cooked. Remove the steamer from the pan, allow the chicken to cool slightly, and cut it into ½-inch to ¾-inch chunks. Add to the potatoes.

Steam the peas 3-5 minutes, or until tender. Remove from the heat and refresh under cold running water. Add to the potatoes and chicken.

Pour the Citrus Tarragon Vinaigrette over the potatoes, chicken, and peas, and mix gently but thoroughly. Season with salt and pepper. Serve at room temperature or chilled.

Serves 4-6

Note: This salad is also wonderful made with fresh asparagus cut into 1-inch sections and steamed just until tender.

Citrus Tarragon Vinaigrette
In a blender or whisking by hand in a small bowl, combine the olive oil, vegetable oil, lemon juice, vinegar, ginger, orange peel, and tarragon.

POTATO AND PEA CURRY

1 tablespoon vegetable oil
1 teaspoon black or yellow
  mustard seeds
1 teaspoon whole cumin seeds
1 tablespoon grated fresh
  ginger
1-2 jalapeño chiles, seeded and
  minced
5 medium boiling potatoes,
  peeled and cut into ¾-inch
  cubes
½ teaspoon ground turmeric
¾ cup water
1 cup low-fat plain yogurt
2 tablespoons cornstarch
1 teaspoon salt
1½ cups fresh or frozen
  shelled peas
chopped cilantro, optional

*T*his is a simple curry that has a creamy yogurt sauce. Since yogurt curdles when it cooks, one of the many useful things that I have learned from Madhur Jaffrey's fine cookbooks is that yogurt can be stabilized for cooking by adding a starch to it.

A curry dinner is enhanced by a variety of accompaniments. This dish is lovely with saffron rice, a fresh tomato chutney, and slices of fresh fruit.

In a large, heavy-bottomed frying pan with a lid, heat the oil over medium-high heat. When hot, add the mustard seeds, partially cover, and cook until they begin to pop, about 30 seconds. Add the cumin, ginger, and chiles, and cook 30 seconds. Add the potatoes and turmeric, stirring to combine with the spices. Lower the heat, add the water and cover tightly. Simmer gently 10-15 minutes, or until the potatoes are tender.

While the potatoes are cooking, scoop the yogurt into a small bowl. Whisk in the cornstarch and salt, making sure there are no lumps.

When the potatoes are tender, add the peas and cook 2-3 minutes. Pour in the yogurt mixture, stirring to distribute evenly. Bring to a simmer over medium heat, and if necessary, add water to thin. Lower the heat and simmer 2 minutes. Serve hot, adding more salt if necessary. If desired, garnish with cilantro.

Serves 4-6

Note: There are a number of ways to grate fresh ginger. Specialized ceramic ginger graters are available commercially. These seem to have taken the place of what I use, a bamboo grater that I bought years ago in San Francisco's Chinatown. If you have a metal grater, you can use the rough section commonly used for citrus peel along with a little brush to make it easier to remove the grated ginger.

One method that requires nothing but a heavy, sharp knife or cleaver is to cut a section of ginger root into thin slices. With the back of the knife, strike the slices to break up the tough fiber, then mince. To peel or not depends upon the tenderness of the skin and the temperament of the cook.

Potato and Pea Curry
(recipe this page)

Baked Goods

Scallion Scones
(recipe on page 156)

SCALLION SCONES

2½ cups mashed potatoes
    (3 medium potatoes)
2 tablespoons butter, melted
3 tablespoons minced
    scallions, green and white
    parts
¾ teaspoon salt
½ teaspoon freshly ground
    black pepper
2 eggs, beaten
1 cup flour
½ teaspoon baking powder
1 teaspoon butter
1 teaspoon oil

These tasty wedges are scones in shape only. Rather than baked, they are pan-fried to a deep golden crust. Because they contain more potatoes than flour, they are like a cross between potato cakes and baked scones. They are wonderful for a brunch or a leisurely Sunday breakfast, especially if you make them up ahead of time and reheat them on a baking sheet 10 minutes at 350°F. (Photo on page 154.)

In a medium bowl, mix the mashed potatoes, butter, scallions, salt, and pepper with a potato masher or wooden spoon. Stir in the eggs. In a small bowl, combine the flour and baking powder, mix well, then stir into the potato mixture to form a sticky dough. Chill at least 1 hour.

Divide the dough into 2 equal portions, and refrigerate the second portion until ready to use. On a well-floured surface, turn out the first dough portion. With floured hands or a well-floured rolling pin, pat or roll the dough into a circle ½ inch thick. With a long knife coated with flour, cut the circle into 4 equal wedges.

In a large nonstick frying pan, heat ½ teaspoon each of the butter and oil over medium-low heat. When hot, transfer the wedges to the pan with a sharp-edged pie server or spatula. Cook slowly 7-10 minutes, turning once, or until deep golden brown on each side.

Repeat with the second portion of dough. Serve the scones hot.

Yields 8 scones

POTATO·CHIVE BISCUITS

2 cups pastry flour, or 1¾ cups
    all-purpose flour
2 teaspoons baking powder
½ teaspoon baking soda
½ teaspoon salt
¼ cup chilled butter
1 cup mashed potatoes
    (1 large potato)
¼ cup low-fat plain yogurt
½ cup low-fat milk
2-3 tablespoons minced chives,
    or minced scallions

I'm sure that most quick bread recipes using potatoes were originally devised by resourceful housewives with leftover mashed potatoes in the larder or when faced with a scarcity of wheat flour. When potatoes are added to a dough, they add moistness and increase the keeping qualities. I love these biscuits with soup and a salad for a Sunday night supper. (Photo on page 78.)

Preheat the oven to 425°F.

In a medium bowl, mix the flour, baking powder, baking soda, and salt. Cut the butter into ¼-inch slices, add to the flour mixture, and cut in with a pastry blender until the mixture resembles coarse cornmeal. Add the potatoes and cut in until the mixture resembles coarse crumbs.

In a small bowl, whisk together the yogurt, milk, and chives. Add all at once to the flour mixture, then stir about 30 seconds. Turn the dough onto a floured board and knead gently and quickly 30 seconds. If necessary, add more flour to prevent sticking. Pat or roll out the dough with a floured rolling pin to a thickness of ¾ inch. Using a 2½-inch biscuit cutter, cut out the biscuits, then place them on a baking sheet 1 inch apart. Bake 12-15 minutes, or until lightly browned. Serve hot.

Yields 10-12 biscuits

Note: For the yogurt and milk mixture, you can substitute ¾ cup buttermilk or ¾ cup milk with 1 tablespoon lemon juice or vinegar.

LEFSA

3 cups riced potatoes or cold
    mashed potatoes put
    through a ricer (3 large
    potatoes)
1 teaspoon salt
¼ cup vegetable oil
1 cup flour, approximately
jam or applesauce for filling

Lefsa are light and delicate potato crepes from Norway. All the recipes that I've read for them refer to the fact that a cook's skill was often judged by the quality of her lefsa. The dough is difficult to handle (a bit like handling spider webs), but it gets easier with each one. The results are always worth the toil. Rolled up with jam or applesauce, lefsa are a lovely dessert. They are also good with cottage cheese and dill.

Place the potatoes in a large bowl and stir in the salt and oil. Gradually stir in enough flour to make a soft dough. (The less flour used, the lighter the *lefsa* will be.) On a large square of waxed paper, form the dough into a cylinder 12 inches long, then wrap it with the waxed paper. Chill at least 2 hours.

Unroll the dough, and with a sharp knife, cut it into 16 equal portions. On a well-floured pastry cloth or waxed paper, pat out with lightly floured hands and then roll out each piece into a 5-inch to 6-inch circle with a lightly floured, stocking-covered rolling pin.

Heat a lightly oiled large nonstick frying pan over medium-high heat. When hot, transfer each *lefsa* to it, and cook one at a time, 2-3 minutes on each side, or until lightly browned. Spread each *lefsa* with jam or applesauce and roll it up. Serve warmed or at room temperature.

Yields 16 lefsa

Note: If your mashed potatoes have a lot of butter in them, cut back on the amount of oil called for in this recipe.

Lefsa *(recipe this page)*

POTATO-OLIVE BREAD

¾ cup all-purpose flour
¾ cup whole-wheat flour
1½ teaspoons baking powder
½ teaspoon salt
¼ cup freshly grated Parmesan
  cheese
¼ cup roughly chopped green
  or black olives
1 large clove garlic, minced
1 cup mashed potatoes
  (1 large potato)
1 large egg, beaten
¼ cup beer or ale

This crusty little loaf is a perfect meal-sized offering for a bread-loving household of four; if discretion is used it will serve six to eight. In the unlikely event that there is any left the next morning, it makes dandy toast for breakfast. I like to use brined green or kalamata olives because of their robust flavor. (Photo on page 85.)

Preheat the oven to 375°F.

In a medium bowl, combine the flours, baking powder, and salt, mixing well. Stir in the cheese, olives, and garlic. In another bowl, combine the potatoes and egg, then stir into the flour mixture. Add the beer all at once and stir well 30 seconds.

Turn the dough out onto a floured surface and knead gently 30 seconds. Form the dough into a 5-inch round loaf, and with a sharp knife, slash a shallow X across the top from side to side, dividing the loaf into four equal quadrants.

Transfer the loaf to a baking sheet and bake 45 minutes, or until golden brown. Place on a wire rack to cool.

Yields 1 loaf

Note: This recipe is easily multiplied to make extra loaves to freeze or for gifts.

SPUD MUFFINS

1¼ cups all-purpose flour
¾ cup yellow cornmeal
1 tablespoon sugar
2 teaspoons baking powder
1 teaspoon salt
½ cup of ¼-inch diced
    Cheddar or Monterey Jack
    cheese
1 cup mashed potatoes
    (1 large potato)
½ cup milk
¼ cup plain yogurt
¼ cup vegetable oil
1 large egg, beaten
1 Anaheim or Hungarian hot
    wax chile, seeded and
    minced
2 scallions, green and white
    parts, minced (⅓ cup)

*T*hese muffins are bursting with flavor and feature a marvelous texture. The flavor comes from scallions, mild chiles, and nuggets of cheese, while the texture comes from a bit of cornmeal and mashed potato added to the dough. Mashed potato in a bread dough or batter provides a deliciously moist crumb.

Preheat the oven to 400°F. Oil the bottom and sides of twelve 2½-inch muffin cups.

In a large bowl, combine the flour, cornmeal, sugar, baking powder, and salt. Add the cheese and dredge with the flour mix, making sure each piece is separate and flour coated.

In a small bowl, use a fork or an electric mixer to beat together the potatoes, milk, yogurt, oil, and egg. Add the chiles and scallions and stir to combine.

Stir the potato mixture into the flour mixture until just blended; the batter will be stiff. With a large spoon, fill each muffin cup nearly to the brim.

Bake 20 minutes, or until the muffins are lightly browned. Remove from the pans and transfer to a basket. Serve hot.

Yields 12 muffins

FOCACCIA DELUXE

Dough

2 tablespoons chopped fresh
    rosemary, or 1 tablespoon
    dried
1 cup boiling water
1 package dry yeast
    (2½ teaspoons)
1 teaspoon sugar
1 teaspoon salt
1¼ cups whole-wheat flour
1 tablespoon olive oil
1-1½ cups white-bread flour

Topping

¾ cup oil-packed sun-dried
    tomatoes, oil reserved
1 tablespoon olive oil
2 medium potatoes, cut into
    ¼-inch cubes
2 large cloves garlic, minced
¼ cup roughly chopped
    kalamata olives
salt and freshly ground black
    pepper, to taste
½ cup freshly grated Parmesan
    cheese

This is a special-occasion bread. It is redolent with rosemary and features an irresistably savory topping of tiny cubes of potato sautéed in olive oil with sun-dried tomatoes and kalamata olives.

For the dough, place the rosemary in a large, heatproof bowl and pour the boiling water over it. When the water has reached a temperature that is comfortably warm to the inside of the wrist, stir in the yeast and sugar. Set aside 10 minutes.

In a small bowl, mix the salt and whole-wheat flour, then stir into the yeast mixture, along with the oil. Gradually add the white flour, ¼ cup at a time. Add only enough to make a soft dough that pulls away from the side of the bowl. Turn the dough out onto a well-floured surface and knead 5 minutes, or until it is smooth and springy. As you knead, add just enough flour to keep the dough from sticking.

Oil a large bowl and place the dough in it, turning it to oil both sides. Cover the bowl with a damp dish towel and place in a warm spot 1½ hours, or until the dough has doubled in size.

For the topping, in a large frying pan, heat 1 tablespoon of the oil from the tomatoes and the olive oil over medium heat. Add the potatoes, and sauté, stirring occasionally,

about 8 minutes. Add the garlic and sauté 2 minutes. Chop the tomatoes, then add them and the olives to the pan, stirring to mix well. Remove from the heat.

Preheat the oven to 375°F.

When the dough has risen, punch it down and transfer it to a lightly floured surface. Pat it into a circle and with a lightly floured rolling pin, roll it into a 12-inch circle. Transfer the dough to a large, oiled baking sheet or pizza pan.

Spoon the topping onto the dough, distributing evenly. Pat the topping firmly into the surface of the dough. Season with salt and pepper. (Because of the saltiness of the olives and cheese, use less salt than usual.) Sprinkle the cheese evenly over the topping.

Bake on the upper shelf of the oven about 25 minutes. Cut into wedges and serve warm.

Yields one 12-inch focaccia

Focaccia Deluxe (recipe this page)

METRIC CONVERSIONS

Dry Weights

U.S. Measurements	Metric Equivalents
¼ ounce	7 grams
⅓ ounce	10 grams
½ ounce	14 grams
1 ounce	28 grams
1½ ounces	42 grams
1¾ ounces	50 grams
2 ounces	57 grams
3 ounces	85 grams
3½ ounces	100 grams
4 ounces (¼ pound)	114 grams
6 ounces	170 grams
8 ounces (½ pound)	227 grams
9 ounces	250 grams
16 ounces (1 pound)	464 grams

Liquid Weights

U.S. Measurements	Metric Equivalents
¼ teaspoon	1.23 ml
½ teaspoon	2.5 ml
¾ teaspoon	3.7 ml
1 teaspoon	5 ml
1 dessertspoon	10 ml
1 tablespoon (3 teaspoons)	15 ml
2 tablespoons (1 ounce)	30 ml
¼ cup	60 ml
⅓ cup	80 ml
½ cup	120 ml
⅔ cup	160 ml
¾ cup	180 ml
1 cup (8 ounces)	240 ml
2 cups (1 pint)	480 ml
3 cups	720 ml
4 cups (1 quart)	1 liter
4 quarts (1 gallon)	3¾ liters

Length

U.S. Measurements	Metric Equivalents
⅛ inch	3 mm
¼ inch	6 mm
⅜ inch	1 cm
½ inch	1.2 cm
1 inch	2.5 cm
¾ inch	2 cm
1¼ inches	3.1 cm
1½ inches	3.7 cm
2 inches	5 cm
3 inches	7.5 cm
4 inches	10 cm
5 inches	12.5 cm

Temperatures

Fahrenheit	Celsius (Centigrade)
32°F (water freezes)	0°C
200°F	95°C
212°F (water boils)	100°C
250°F	120°C
275°F	135°C
300°F (slow oven)	150°C
325°F	160°C
350°F (moderate oven)	175°C
375°F	190°C
400°F (hot oven)	205°C
425°F	220°C
450°F (very hot oven)	230°C
475°F	245°C
500°F (extremely hot oven)	260°C

SOURCES

Moose Tubers
P.O. Box 520
Waterville, ME 04903-0520
(207) 873-7333
Moose Tubers is part of Fedco Seeds. They offer a large number of well-described varieties, as well as several seed potato sampler collections. All of their seed potatoes are certified; many of them are also certified organically grown. The free Fedco catalog also offers a wide range of vegetable and flower seeds, cover crops, and gardening suppplies.

Ronnigers
P.O. Box 307
Ellensburg, WA 98926
(800) 846-6178
Ronnigers was founded in the mid-1980s by potato grower David Ronniger and has been influential in introducing the general public to a wealth of unusual potato varieties. In 1997, Ronnigers came under new ownership and will offer both certified and organically grown stock. They have a large selection of garlic, shallots, onions, and other alliums with extensive cultivation instructions for these as well as for potatoes. Free catalog.

Seed Savers Exchange
3076 North Winn Road
Decorah, IA 52101
(319) 382-5872
This worthy organization is a network of members interested in the preservation of traditional open-pollinated seeds, as well as potatoes and other

tubers. Membership brings three fascinating and informative publications a year, one of them a 320-page book of seeds, fruit tree scions, and tubers available from members. Membership is $25. There is also a special $15 or $20 membership fee (no questions asked) for those with reduced incomes. Source for Charlotte, Gold Nugget, and Siberian.

Snow Pond Farm Supply
RR 2, Box 4075
Belgrade, ME 04917
(800) 768-9998
Potatoes are the heart of Snow Pond's business. Their informative free catalog has a large selection of certified seed, much of it certified organically grown. Snow Pond also offers an extensive variety of cover crops accompanied by a detailed and educational text, as well as gardening and small-scale farming supplies and books.

Wood Prairie Farm
49 Kinney Road
Bridgewater, ME 04735
(800) 829-9765
Organic growers Jim and Megan Gerritsen specialize in potatoes. They offer about 16 varieties as certified seed potatoes, and from September to April they ship out their wares in their Maine Potato Sampler of the Month Club. Wood Prairie Farm also offers a line of potato postcards and a supply of organic vegetables and grains by mail. Free catalog.

BIBLIOGRAPHY

Blalock, Cecilia. "The Potato Planet." *Frozen Food Report*. Spring 1997, 28-31.

Brody, Jane. *Jane Brody's Good Food Book*. New York: Bantam, 1987.

Bubel, Nancy, and Mike Bubel. *Root Cellaring*. Pownal, Vt.: Storey Communications, 1991.

Capon, Brian. *Botany for Gardeners*. Portland, Ore.: Timber Press, 1990.

Child, Julia. *The Way to Cook*. New York: Alfred A. Knopf, 1989.

Fisher, M. F. K. *How to Cook a Wolf*. New York: Farrar, Straus & Giroux, 1988.

Greene, Janet, et al. *Putting Food By*, 4th ed. Lexington, Mass.: The Stephen Greene Press, 1988.

Heiser, Charles B. *The Fascinating World of the Nightshades*. New York: Dover, 1987.

Hirsch, David. *The Moosewood Restaurant Kitchen Garden*. New York: Simon & Schuster, 1992.

Hobhouse, Henry. *Seeds of Change*. New York: Harper and Row, 1987.

Kinealy, Christine. *This Great Calamity, The Irish Famine 1845-52*. Boulder, Colo.: Roberts Rinehart, 1995.

La Place, Viana. *Verduras*. New York: William Morrow, 1991.

McGee, Harold. *On Food and Cooking*. New York: Collier Books, 1988.

The Moosewood Collective. *New Recipes from Moosewood Restaurant*. Berkeley, Calif.: Ten Speed Press, 1987.

Mott, Lawrie, and Karen Snyder. *Pesticide Alert: A Guide to Pesticides in Fruits and Vegetables*. San Francisco: Sierra Club, 1987.

Napolitano, Pete. *Produce Pete's Farmacopeia*. New York: Hearst Books, 1994.

Phillips, Roger, and Martyn Rix. *The Random House Book of Vegetables*. New York: Random House, 1993.

Potato Field Manual. Pocatello, Idaho: J. R. Simplot Company, 1985.

Root, Waverley. *Food*. New York: Konecky and Konecky, 1980.

Russell, Howard S. *A Long, Deep Furrow: Three Centuries of Farming in New England*. Hanover, N.H.: University Press of New England, 1982.

Salaman, Redcliffe. *The History and Social Influence of the Potato*. Cambridge, England: Cambridge University Press, 1985.

Simpson, Beryl, and Molly Ogorzaly. *Economic Botany: Plants in Our World*. New York: McGraw-Hill, 1995.

Smith, Bruce D. *The Emergence of Agriculture*. New York: W. H. Freeman and Co., 1995.

Viola, Herman, and Carolyn Margolis. *Seeds of Change*. Washington, D.C.: Smithsonian Institution Press, 1991.

Waldron, Maggie. *Potatoes, A Country Garden Cookbook*. San Francisco: Collins Publishers, 1993.

Whealey, Kent, comp. *Garden Seed Inventory*. 4th ed. Decorah, Iowa: Seed Saver Publications, 1995.

INDEX

BOOK PUBLISHER: Jim Childs

ASSOCIATE PUBLISHER: Helen Albert

EDITORIAL ASSISTANT: Cherilyn DeVries

EDITOR: Diane Sinitsky

DESIGNER: Jodie Delohery

LAYOUT ARTIST: Michael Mandarano

PHOTOGRAPHERS (except where noted): Boyd Hagen: cover, pages 5 (bottom), 6, 9, 34 (left), 41, 43, 47, 48, 50, 51, 52, 53, 54, 58, 64, 69, 72, 78, 85, 88, 94, 102, 107, 108, 115, 120, 124, 128, 133, 135, 139, 144, 149, 152, 154, 158, 163;
David Cavagnaro: pages 5 (top), 11, 15, 17, 19, 20, 21, 22, 23, 24, 25, 26, 27, 28, 29, 31, 32, 33, 34 (right), 35, 36, 37, 39, 42, 44, 45

ILLUSTRATOR: Rosalie Vaccaro

RECIPE TESTER: Connie Welch

ART DIRECTOR FOR FOOD PHOTOGRAPHY: Henry Roth

FOOD STYLIST: Abigail Johnson Dodge

PROP STYLIST: Sheila F. Shulman
Props supplied by Pier One, Pottery Barn, Kaplan and Associates

TYPEFACE: Berling

PAPER: 70-lb. Somerset Gloss

PRINTER: R. R. Donnelley, Willard, Ohio